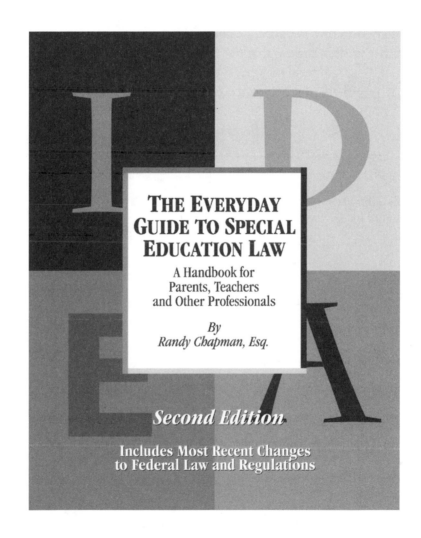

THE EVERYDAY GUIDE TO SPECIAL EDUCATION LAW

A Handbook for
Parents, Teachers
and Other Professionals

By
Randy Chapman, Esq.

Second Edition

**Includes Most Recent Changes
to Federal Law and Regulations**

The Everyday Guide to Special Education Law
Handbook for Parents, Teachers and Other Professionals
By Randy Chapman, Esq.

Copyright © 2008 The Legal Center for People with Disabilities and Older People
455 Sherman Street, Suite 130
Denver, Colorado 80203

This publication is designed to provide accurate and general information in regard to the subject matter covered. It is sold with the understanding that the author and the publisher are not engaged in rendering legal or other professional services.
If specific legal advice is required, please consult an attorney.

Second Edition
Second Printing 2010

Publisher's Cataloging-In-Publication Data
(Prepared by The Donohue Group, Inc.)

Chapman, Randy.
  The everyday guide to special education law : a handbook for parents, teachers and other professionals / by Randy Chapman. -- 2nd ed.

     p. ; cm.

  "Includes most recent changes to federal law and legislation."
  Includes index.
  ISBN: 978-0-9770179-3-5

1. United States. Individuals with Disabilities Education Improvement Act of 2004--Handbooks, manuals, etc. 2. United States. Individuals with Disabilities Education Act--Handbooks, manuals, etc. 3. United States. Americans with Disabilities Act of 1990--Handbooks, manuals, etc. 4. United States. Rehabilitation Act of 1973--Handbooks, manuals, etc. 5. Special education--Law and legislation--United States--Handbooks, manuals, etc. 6. Children with disabilities--Education--Law and legislation--United States--Handbooks, manuals, etc. I. Title.

KF4209.3.Z9 C453 2008
344.0791   2008927540

Book and Cover Design by MacGraphics Services
Front Cover Concept by John O. Kjos and Randy Chapman
Edited by Joyce Miller, Integrated Writer Services
Production coordinated by Julie Z. Busby, Randy Chapman and Mary Anne Harvey
Indexing by Katie Banks, Eagle-Eye Indexing
Printing by United Graphics, Inc.

Lead Sponsors

DANIELS FUND
Making life better…one individual at a time.

ROSE
COMMUNITY FOUNDATION

Gold Sponsors

GIBSON, DUNN & CRUTCHER LLP

Silver Sponsors

Sam S. Bloom Foundation

THE SCHRAMM FOUNDATION

FIRST DATA FOUNDATION
WESTERN UNION

CHBA
Colorado Hispanic Bar Association

Colorado Developmental Disabilities Council

Gannett Foundation
9NEWS
Where News Comes First

Table of Contents

Preface

I wrote this book primarily to help students, parents, advocates, and other professionals better understand the Individuals with Disabilities Education Act (IDEA). Congress, most recently, amended the IDEA in 2004. Subsequently, the Department of Education adopted regulations implementing the IDEA 2004 that were effective July 5, 2006. This edition of The Everyday Guide addresses the major changes in the IDEA 2004 including references to the Department of Education regulations. The IDEA statute is very detailed and, for the most part, the regulations follow the statute without adding much clarification. So, I have only referred to the regulations where I thought they provided additional information or clarified the statute. I have also tried to make the law a little less confusing.

By saying I wrote this book primarily for students, parents, and advocates, I don't mean that it isn't also intended for teachers and other educators. Most teachers and educators advocate for children with disabilities, in general, and their own students, in particular. They just advocate from within the educational system. So, while the book is written from a parent perspective, the information is also intended to help those who have answered the call to become a member of that most honorable of professions, teachers.

This book is not intended to be a legal treatise on special education case law. The book is meant to be an everyday guide to special education law to help parents, advocates, students with disabilities, and educators to understand the basic requirements of the IDEA, Section 504 of the Rehabilitation Act of 1973 and Title II of the Americans with Disabilities Act.

School services for children with disabilities are developed through an individualized planning process. The planning process involves parents, educators, and other professionals. For infants and toddlers that process results in an Individualized Family Service Plan (IFSP) and for children aged three to twenty-one that process results in an Individualized Educational Program (IEP). The IFSP and IEP meetings should involve a collaborative process.

Generally, I do not believe the IEP, IFSP, and other education meetings are the appropriate settings for lawyers and others to debate legal standards and court rulings. Those debates are more appropriate for due process hearings and court cases. Educational planning meetings should focus on the student's needs and meeting those needs. Parents, teachers, and other professionals know about the individual students and how to teach students with disabilities. Early intervention service providers and families have expertise on providing early intervention services to infants and toddlers. While parents and teachers should understand the legal requirements in the special education process, they are not in the planning meeting to be lawyers. They are in the meeting to be parents and teachers. I believe parents and educators—not attorneys—should design educational programs.

Having said that parents and educators—not attorneys—should design programs, I would also like to point out that there is certainly a role for attorneys to play in ensuring that students receive a free appropriate public education under the IDEA. Disputes often arise over the delivery of special education services. While most disputes can be resolved informally without involving lawyers, some require more formal dispute resolution procedures like due process hearings. While parents are not required to use attorneys in due process proceedings, due process hearings are formal legal proceedings and school districts are most likely represented by attorneys.

Consequently, parents will likely need representation by an attorney. Moreover, parents may need to seek advice from an attorney to make decisions regarding dispute resolution. Although this book contains information about the legal rights of students with disabilities, it is not a substitute for legal advice or legal representation when either is needed. The book is best used as a guide to the law and the rights of students with disabilities to get a free appropriate public education. If legal advice is needed, it should be sought from an attorney competent in this area of the law.

Additionally, please note that in some places I have directly quoted the law. **But in many places, I have modified and paraphrased the legal language to make it more understandable.** Footnotes are provided so you can find the actual statute or regulation being discussed. The IDEA statute is cited as 20 U.S.C. 1400 to 1487. The IDEA regulations are 34 CFR Part 300. You can find the IDEA statute and regulations at the United States Department of Education website http:\\idea.ed.gov. The Section 504 regulations are cited as 34 C.F.R. Part 104. The letters U.S.C. stand for United States Code and C.F.R. stands for Code of Federal Regulations. **If you are seeking to quote the law exactly, you should use these footnotes to find your exact quote, rather than quoting this book.**

Additionally, a glossary is provided as Appendix D. Terms that are defined in the glossary appear in *italics* the first time they appear in this book.

Finally, I greatly enjoyed writing this book and hope it's helpful.

Randy Chapman

Randy Chapman

Acknowledgments

Many people helped produce this book. I would like to acknowledge the contributions of the following staff members of The Legal Center for People with Disabilities and Older People. Thanks to Mary Anne Harvey, our Executive Director, for her support, suggestions, and, as always, excellent editing skills. I would also like to thank Bill Higgins, the Managing Attorney in The Legal Center's Grand Junction office; Thom Miller, Special Education Program Coordinator; Heidi Van Huysen, Special Education Attorney; Angie Garberding, Rights Advocate; and Julie Busby, Office Manager. Thanks also to Diane Carabello, our Director of Development, who helped find funding to support this project.

Thanks also to Chug Roberts of TheCapitol. Net in Alexandria, Virginia, for his consultation and encouragement, and to Mandy M. Rigg for her enthusiastic support and advice.

Additionally, I want to thank the following people who also reviewed drafts of this book and provided invaluable insight and suggestions: Allison Seyler and Shirley Swope with the PEAK Parent Training Center in Colorado Springs; Romie Tobin, who as a parent advocated for her son and now helps other parents; Dr. Fred Smokoski, who is a former Director of Special Education in Colorado and helped bring students from the Wheat Ridge State Home and Training School into the public schools; Susan Smith with Colorado Department of Education; Julie Haynes with the Colorado Foundation for Families and Children; Patricia S. Tomlan, Ph.D., with PST Educational Consultants; and Carol Meredith, Cg LaScala and Paula A. House with the Arc/Arapahoe & Douglas.

We are grateful to the Colorado Developmental Disabilities Council for funding this project. In addition, we extend our gratitude to the Daniels Fund for a challenge grant to encourage charitable support to broadly distribute this book to families who need it and make it available in Spanish.

Last but not least, I want to acknowledge Carol, Connor, and Sean Chapman who patiently tolerated my hogging the "computer room" while writing this book.

Mary Anne Harvey and I
would especially like to acknowledge
John Matousek of our Board of Directors
for nurturing the entrepreneurial spirit
that will sustain our future.

Introduction

In 1980 The Legal Center for Handicapped Citizens and the Association for Retarded Citizens in Colorado sued the Colorado Department of Education because children at the Wheat Ridge State Home and Training School were not attending school. The Wheat Ridge State Home and Training School (Ridge) was an institution for persons with developmental disabilities located in the Jefferson County School District. Most of the children living in the institution originally came from a variety of communities and school districts, other than the Jefferson County School District. Abandoned, today, the wards at Ridge are empty. But in 1980, children filled wards labeled *Moonbeam*, *Aspen*, and *Starlight*. Filled wards, empty days.

Ridge students had the right to an education under the Education for All Handicapped Children Act of 1975.[1] The Legal Center had first discovered in 1979 that children living at Ridge were not going to school. Consequently, on behalf of the parents of several of the children living at Ridge, The Legal Center requested school services from the children's home school districts, specifically the Denver, Boulder, and Weld County districts. These home school districts, however, refused to provide school services because the children lived in Jefferson County. The Legal Center then turned to the Jefferson County School District for services, but services were refused because the children's parents resided outside of Jefferson County.

Since the Education for All Handicapped Children Act required that the State Education Agency (the Colorado Department of Education) assure that all children with disabilities in Colorado receive a free appropriate public education, The Legal Center implored Colorado's Commissioner of Education to resolve which school districts were responsible for teaching these children. Eventually, the Commissioner of Education determined that the school districts where the children's parents resided were responsible for educating children living at Ridge. Unfortunately, that decision was not enforced; the children stayed out of school.

Consequently, the class action lawsuit was filed in 1980 in federal district court in Denver. In May 1981 Judge John Kane ruled that, in fact, the Commissioner of Education and the Colorado Department of Education were responsible under the Education for All Handicapped Children Act of 1975 for assuring that all children with disabilities in Colorado, including the children at Ridge, receive a free appropriate public education.[2] The lawsuit was later settled, and

---

[1] The Legal Center for Handicapped Citizens is now called The Legal Center for People with Disabilities and Older People, the Association for Retarded Citizens in Colorado is now called The Arc of Colorado and the Education for All Handicapped Children Act is now called the Individuals with Disabilities Education Act or the IDEA.

[2] *Association for Retarded Citizens in Colorado v. Frazier*, 517 F. Supp. 105 (D.Co. 1981)

in the fall of 1981 children at the Ridge State Home and Training School attended school for the first time. At the same time, school services were also provided to children living at Colorado's other State Home and Training Schools in Pueblo and Grand Junction. For awhile, some children received school services at the State Home and Training School, but nearly one half of the children left the institution and attended schools in their home district.

Many of these children had very severe disabilities. Some were unable to speak or walk. For the first time children with very severe disabilities received services in Colorado's public schools. Over time, this lawsuit directly resulted in improving the ability of Colorado's public schools to serve children with severe disabilities. This improvement, in turn, led to closing almost all of the segregated schools in Colorado, children leaving the institutions, and children with severe disabilities being more fully included in the public school system. All of these changes came about because of the Education for All Handicapped Children Act!

The Education for All Handicapped Children Act was adopted by Congress in 1975. Congress passed the law because nationwide children with disabilities were either excluded from the public schools (like the children at Ridge), or provided minimal educational services. Initially, the courts confronted the exclusion of children from the public schools through the civil rights movement. In 1954, the Supreme Court ruled in *Brown v. Board of Education* that segregating children in the public schools based on their race violated the 14th Amendment of the Constitution. Racial segregation in the public schools denied children an equal access to a public education.[3] Later, other parents pressed for equal access to the public schools for their children with disabilities.

Armed with the *Brown* decision, parent advocacy groups also chose the courts as a battleground to get school services for their children with disabilities. In 1972 two landmark decisions, *Pennsylvania Association for Retarded Children v. Commonwealth of Pennsylvania*[4] and *Mills v. D.C. Board of Education*,[5] determined that children with disabilities must have equal access to public education, and parents must have a meaningful opportunity to challenge decisions excluding their children from school. Although these two decisions led the charge, there were court cases in other states seeking school services for children with disabilities.

In 1975 Congress passed Public Law 94-142, the Education for All Handicapped Children Act, which is now called the Individuals with

> Sadly, Congress further found that "more than half of the handicapped children in the United States do not receive appropriate educational services which would enable them to have full educational opportunity," and "one million of the handicapped children in the United States are excluded entirely from the public school system and will not go through the educational process with their peers.

---

[3] 347 U.S. 483 (1954)
[4] 334 F. Supp. 1257 (E.D. Pa. 1971, 343 F. Supp. 279 (E.D. Pa. 1972)
[5] 348 F. Supp. 866 (D.D.C.1972)

Disabilities Education Act or the IDEA.[6] In passing the law, Congress found that there were "more than eight million handicapped children in the United States."[7]

Sadly, Congress further found that "more than half of the handicapped children in the United States do not receive appropriate educational services which would enable them to have full educational opportunity,"[8] and "one million of the handicapped children in the United States **are excluded entirely from the public school system and will not go through the educational process with their peers.**"[9] Note that these Congressional findings documenting the exclusion of children with disabilities from our nation's schools are as recent as 1975. To remedy this national shame, the new law required that children with disabilities receive a free appropriate public education and that special education and related services be provided to children according to an Individualized Educational Program (IEP). Congress had set out to right this great wrong.

In 1990 Congress amended some of the language in the Education for All Handicapped Children Act and changed its name to the Individuals with Disabilities Education Act or

IDEA. Fittingly, throughout the law the term "handicapped children" was replaced with the term "children with disabilities." In 1997 Congress reauthorized and amended the IDEA, and then in March 1999, the U.S. Department of Education issued new regulations interpreting the amended IDEA.[10] The IDEA 97 was the first major revision of the law since its original passage as the Education for All Handicapped Children Act in 1975. The law was again amended in 2004.

Without question, this federal legislation improved the lives of millions of children with disabilities throughout the country. Many of the children, initially served by the law in the late 1970s and early 1980s, are now high school and college graduates. Many are employed in careers; some, without doubt, are teachers, and many are now parents themselves. Without this law all of those opportunities would have been denied to these IDEA graduates, just as they had been denied to the children with disabilities who preceded them. As for the students at Ridge, school taught many of them to talk, to walk, and to live more independently. Because of the IDEA, all of the children from Ridge finally attended school.

---

[6]   20 U.S.C. 1400
[7]   20 U.S.C. 1400 (b)(1) (1975)
[8]   20 U.S.C. 1400 (b)(3) (1975)
[9]   20 U.S.C. 1400 (b)(4) (1975) emphasis supplied.
[10] 34 C.F.R. Parts 300 and 303

Dedication

*This book is dedicated
to all of the graduates
of the Wheat Ridge State Home
and Training School.*

I   The Individuals with Disabilities Education Act

All kids get to go to school and get a fair chance to learn. That's the idea behind the IDEA. All kids get to go to school and get a fair chance to learn. Kids, including kids with disabilities, go to school with their neighbors. Kids, including kids with disabilities, sit in classrooms together. Kids, including kids with disabilities, join school clubs, go to assemblies, go on field trips, go to school plays, and go to school sports events. Kids are not separated in school because they have a disability. All kids get to go to school. All the words written by Congress, when enacting and reenacting the IDEA, support that simple idea.

Getting a fair chance to learn, for kids with disabilities, means getting school services that meet their individual needs. To meet individual needs, schools provide specially designed instruction. Providing specially designed instruction means adapting and modifying what and how schools teach. To make sure services

are individualized, schools provide services according to an *individualized educational program*. All of this is done to make sure kids with disabilities get a fair chance to learn. Congress calls this providing a *free appropriate public education*. Congress reauthorized the IDEA in 2004, making sure kids with disabilities continue receiving that education.

In enacting the IDEA 97, Congress strengthened the IDEA's requirements regarding providing students with disabilities access to the general educational curriculum in regular classrooms, added *parents* and regular education teachers to the IEP team, and added provisions for disciplining students with disabilities while ensuring their right to a free appropriate education.

> All kids get to go to school and get a fair chance to learn. That's the idea behind the IDEA.

In 2004 Congress again reauthorized the IDEA. In the IDEA 2004, Congress continued to emphasize and strengthen the participation of parents and families in their children's education, continued to emphasize the importance of providing students with disabilities access to the general curriculum and educating students in the regular classroom, encouraged flexibility in the IEP process, tried to remove unnecessary paperwork burdens on educators, and expanded dispute resolution procedures to encourage positive dispute resolution.

In 2004 just as it had done twenty-nine years before, Congress declared its reasons for reauthorizing the IDEA. First, Congress stated that: "Disability is a natural part of the human experience and in no way diminishes the right of individuals to participate in or contribute to society. Improving educational results for children with disabilities is an essential element of our national policy of ensuring equality of opportunity, full participation, independent living, and economic self-sufficiency for individuals with disabilities."[11]

Congress then reacknowledged that before the Education of All Handicapped Children Act of 1975 was passed ". . . the educational needs of **millions** of children with disabilities were not being fully met because

1. the children did not receive appropriate educational services;

2. the children were excluded entirely from the public school system and from being educated with their peers;

3. undiagnosed disabilities prevented the children from having a successful educational experience; or

4. a lack of resources within the public school system **forced families** to find service outside the public school system."[12]

Furthermore, Congress found that "almost 30 years of research and experience had demonstrated that the education of children with disabilities can be made more effective by having high expectations of students with disabilities and ensuring those students have access to the general curriculum in the regular classroom, to the maximum extent possible. . ."[13]

Additionally in IDEA 2004, Congress noted the importance of parents in the education process by stating that the education of children with disabilities can be made more effective by "strengthening the role and responsibility of parents and ensuring that families of such children have meaningful opportunities to participate in the education of their children at school and at home."[14]

Additionally in IDEA 2004, Congress noted the importance of parents in the education process by stating that the education of children with disabilities can be made more effective by "strengthening the role and responsibility of parents and ensuring that families of such children have meaningful opportunities to participate in the education of their children at school and at home."

---

[11] 20 U.S.C. 1401(c)(1)
[12] 20 U.S.C. 1401(c)(2) emphasis supplied.
[13] 20 U.S.C. 1401(c)(5)(A)
[14] 20 U.S.C. 1401(c)(5)(B)

Moreover, Congress, concerned that disputes between parents and school districts be resolved more usefully and positively, found that "parents and schools should be given expanded opportunities to resolve their differences in positive and constructive ways."[15]

Finally, Congress stated that the purpose of the IDEA is "to ensure that all children with disabilities have available to them a free appropriate public education that emphasizes special education and related services designed to meet their unique needs and prepare them for further education, employment, and independent living" and to "ensure that the rights of children with disabilities and parents of such children are protected."[16]

Thus, the IDEA's primary directive is the same now as when the Education for All Handicapped Children Act was passed in 1975: all children with disabilities must be provided a free appropriate public education. All kids get to go to school and get a fair chance to learn.

What Is a Free Appropriate Public Education?

Providing a free appropriate public education means providing a student with disabilities **special education** services and the **related services** the student needs to benefit from her special education program. A free appropriate public education requires that services:

1. are provided at public expense, under public supervision and direction, and without charge;

2. meet the standards of the state educational agency;

3. include an appropriate preschool, elementary, or secondary school education; and

4. are provided in conformity with the individualized educational program (IEP).[17]

Educators, advocates, and attorneys who work in the field of special education often use initials/letters or acronyms to refer to frequently used concepts and phrases. The acronym for the term free appropriate public education is FAPE. In this book I will try to identify the acronyms that are used, such as LRE for *least restrictive environment*, ESY for extended school year, and IAES for *interim alternative educational setting*. But I believe that speaking in initials, rather than words, frequently confuses more than it clarifies. So, while I will try to point out the most common acronyms, I won't use most of them in the text. I have also listed the most common acronyms in the Glossary in Appendix D.

In each state the *State Education Agency* (SEA), is responsible for ensuring that all children with disabilities receive a free appropriate public education in that state. Local education agencies (LEAs) are responsible for ensuring that students with disabilities, within the agencies' boundaries, receive a free appropriate public education. Local education agencies are administrative bodies, most often local school districts or a combination of school districts that are responsible for public elementary and secondary schools.[18] In this book, for the sake of simplicity, local education agencies **will usually be referred to as school districts**. School districts have the primary responsibility for providing special education services to students with disabilities.

---

[15] 20 U.S.C. 1401(c)(8)
[16] 20 U.S.C. 1401(d)(1)(A) and (B)
[17] 20 U.S.C. 1402(9)
[18] 20 U.S.C. 1402(19)

Providing an appropriate education also means educating students with disabilities in the least restrictive environment. I will discuss this idea more later, but, generally, the least restrictive environment means students with disabilities learn, in regular classrooms, along side children who do not have disabilities. Schools provide *supplementary aids and services* to support students to succeed in regular classrooms. Students with disabilities are also provided the related services they need to benefit from their special education program. In this book you will learn these terms. Who are children with disabilities? What is special education? What are related services? What are supplementary aids and services? What is the least restrictive environment?

Who Are Children with Disabilities?

The IDEA uses the term children with disabilities to identify students who are eligible for a free appropriate public education. A *child with a disability* means a child with mental retardation, hearing impairments (including deafness), speech or language impairments, visual impairments (including blindness), serious emotional disturbance, orthopedic impairments, autism, traumatic brain injury, other health impairments, or specific learning disabilities; **and who needs**, because of having any of these conditions, **special education and related services**.[19] If a student does not meet this definition, then the student is not eligible for IDEA services.

Note, to be considered a child with a disability, a student must have an impairment **and** need

special education and related services. Some students may have impairments, but may not need special education and related services. In that case, the student is not eligible for services under the IDEA. The student, however, may be eligible for services under section 504 of the Rehabilitation Act. That law is discussed in Chapter VIII. Students are determined eligible for IDEA services through the Individualized Educational Program or IEP process.

In this process, a student is first referred for evaluations to determine whether the student has special needs and is eligible for IDEA services. After the evaluations are completed, an individualized educational program (IEP) team will meet to determine the child's eligibility for special education services. The team is made up of necessary school staff, the child's parents, and, at the parent's or school's discretion, other individuals who know about the student's needs. The IEP team will determine whether the child has an impairment and, if so, whether the child needs special education and related services. If the child needs special education services, as a result of having an impairment, the child will be determined to have a disability and will be eligible for IDEA services. If the team determines that the child has a disability, the IEP team will proceed to complete the IEP.[20]

> Note, to be considered a child with a disability, a student must have an impairment and need special education and related services.

This book discusses two Parts of the IDEA; Part B and Part C. The majority of the book

---

[19] 20 U.S.C. 1402(3)

[20] Please see Chapter IV for a discussion of the IEP process.

discusses Part B. Part B requires that students with disabilities from the ages of 3 to 21 (school age) receive a free appropriate public education. The IDEA's Part C requires *early intervention services* for children from birth through age two (infants and toddlers). Chapter IX discusses the requirements of Part C.

What Is Special Education?

Once the IEP team finds that a student has a disability, the student is entitled to a free appropriate public education. This means the school district must offer the student special education and related services. **Special education** means specially designed instruction, at no cost to parents, to meet the unique needs of a child with a disability, including

1. instruction conducted in the classroom, in the home, in hospitals and institutions, and in other settings; and

2. instruction in physical education.[21]

Schools provide specially designed instruction by adapting the content, methodology, or delivery of instruction to meet the unique needs of the student with a disability. As you will later see, focusing on a student's **unique needs** is important in the IEP process.

The IDEA does not promote placing students in homes, hospitals, and institutions in order to receive instruction. The requirement that students receive instruction in their homes, in hospitals, and in institutions is meant to ensure that if children are in one of those settings, unable to attend school, they still receive educational services. For example, if a student has a lengthy illness and is hospitalized, the school must still educate the student, even though she may not be able to go to school.

Special education services must meet the needs of the individual child. When the IEP team meets and designs a program for a particular child, the team is meeting to discuss that child's needs and program, not the needs of other children in the school district. Certainly, the needs of other children are important and need to be addressed. But the IEP meeting focuses on the needs of one particular student with a disability.

What Are Related Services?

A free appropriate public education includes providing related services that a child needs to benefit from her special education. The term related services includes the early identification and assessment of disabling conditions in children, transportation and developmental, corrective, and other support services such as:

- speech-language pathology and audiology,

- *interpreting services,*

- psychological services,

- physical and occupational therapy,

- recreation *including therapeutic recreation,*

- social work services,

- *school nurse services designed to enable a child with a disability to receive a free appropriate public education as described in the individualized program of the child,*

> A free appropriate public education includes providing related services that a child needs to benefit from her special education.

---

[21] 20 U.S.C. 1402(29)(B)

- counseling services, including rehabilitation counseling, orientation and mobility services, and

- **medical services, except that such medical services shall be for diagnostic and evaluation purposes only.**[22]

[Note that the related services in *italics* were added in IDEA 2004.]

Assistive technology devices and services are one type of related service. Assistive technology devices can be provided as a related service or to support the provision of a particular related service. For example, a student may need access to an augmentative communication device as part of the child's receiving speech therapy services. Similarly, a child may need a standing board to benefit from physical therapy services, or a child may need card holders and adapted toys and games to benefit from recreation services.

Finally, the IDEA 2004 specifically excludes medical devices that are surgically implanted from both the definition of assistive technology device and the definition of related services.[23] This would appear to categorize cochlear implants for individuals with hearing impairments as medical services that are not required to be provided under the IDEA. While school districts are not required to provide surgically implanted devices such as cochlear implants, they must ensure that those devices, as well as hearing aids, are functioning properly. But school districts are not responsible for post-sur-

gical maintenance, programming, or replacement of a surgically implanted device.[24]

Medical Services Versus Related Services

While school districts must provide students the related services they need to benefit from their special education program, school districts are not required to provide medical treatment or medical services to children with disabilities. If the IEP team, however, needs a doctor's diagnosis to determine the student's disability, then the school district must provide that "medical" assessment.

For example, an IEP team may need a neurological evaluation, done by a licensed neurologist, to determine the nature and frequency of a student's seizures. A neurologist is a physician, but since that **medical service** is being done for educational, diagnostic or evaluation purposes, the school district must ensure that it is provided at no cost to the student's parents. The school district is not, however, required to provide neurological treatment for the student, beyond the diagnosis.

The courts have struggled with what is a **related service**, and required to be provided to students with disabilities, versus what is a **medical service**, and only required for diagnostic and evaluation purposes. In the spring of 1999, in *Cedar Rapids Community School District v. Garret F.*, the Supreme Court clarified this troublesome issue.[25]

When Garret F. was four, he was hurt in a motorcycle accident. The accident severed Garret's spinal column leaving him paralyzed from the neck down. Garret attended regular classes in school, was successful academically, but he needed an electric ventilator to breathe and

---

[22] 20 U.S.C. 1402(26) emphasis and italics added. Italics indicate new language added with the IDEA 2004.

[23] 20 U.S.C. 1402(1) and (26)(B)

[24] 34 CFR 300.113

[25] *Cedar Rapids Community School District v. Garret F.*, 526 U.S. 66, 119 S. Ct. 992 (1999)

assistance with urinary bladder catheterization and suctioning of his tracheotomy tube. Garret also needed help from someone familiar with his ventilator, in case there was a malfunction or electrical problem. Without these "nursing services," Garret couldn't go to school.

The Cedar Rapids Community School District agreed these services didn't require a licensed physician, but because of their cost and medical nature, the district refused to provide the services. Garret's parents appealed, eventually reaching the United States Supreme Court.

The Supreme Court determined that the services Garret needed were related services. The Court focused on two points. First, Garret needed these services to remain in school throughout the day. Second, a licensed physician was not required to provide the services. The Court reasoned that related services were services that students need to benefit from special education. On the other hand, medical services are specifically defined as services provided by a licensed physician. In Garret's case, it was clear, he needed these services to go to school. It was also clear, the services did not have to be provided by a licensed medical doctor. Thus, despite their cost and medical nature, the nursing services Garret needed were related services. Consequently, the school district had to provide them.

What Are Supplementary Aids and Services?

Supplementary aids and services are supports that help students with disabilities succeed in regular classrooms. Students with disabilities must be educated, to the maximum extent appropriate, in regular classrooms with students without disabilities. Before placing students

in special classes, separate schools, or otherwise removing students with disabilities from the regular education environment, schools must consider providing supplementary aids and services to support success in the regular classroom.[26] Thus, supplementary aids and services are aids, services, and other supports that are provided in regular education classes, or other education-related settings, to enable students with disabilities to be educated, to the maximum extent appropriate, with students without disabilities.[27]

Supplementary aids and services include modifying and adapting materials for students, and providing additional supports and assistance to the regular education teacher. Providing assistive technology devices and services can help students with disabilities succeed in regular education classrooms and settings. Thus, assistive technology devices and services may also be considered supplementary aids and services.

For example, materials can be adapted so that they are in large print or Braille for students with visual impairments. Frequency Modulation (FM) auditory training devices can assist

> Before placing students in special classes, separate schools, or otherwise removing students with disabilities from the regular education environment, schools must consider providing supplementary aids and services to support success in the regular classroom.

---

[26] 20 U.S.C. 1412(a)(5)
[27] 20 U.S.C. 1402(33)

students with hearing impairments. Providing an augmentative communication device to a student, who cannot speak, would help the student talk with other students and the teacher. These are just a few examples of using supplementary aids or services to help support students with disabilities in the regular classroom. We'll come back to supplementary aids and services, when we discuss least restrictive environment.

What Are Assistive Technology Devices and Services?

We've already touched a little on assistive technology (AT) devices and services. Here's what they are. Assistive technology devices are items and pieces of equipment that are used to increase, maintain, or improve functional capabilities of children with disabilities. Assistive technology services are then defined as any service that directly assists a child in the selection, acquisition, or use of an assistive technology device.[28] Assistive technology services include

1. evaluating the needs of the student, including a functional evaluation of the student in the student's customary environment;

2. purchasing, leasing, or otherwise providing for the acquisition of AT devices for the student;

3. selecting, designing, fitting, customizing, adapting, applying, maintaining, repairing, or replacing of AT devices;

4. coordinating and using other therapies, interventions, or services with AT de-

vices such as those associated with existing education and rehabilitation plans and programs;

5. training or technical assistance for the student, or, where appropriate, the student's family; and

6. training or technical assistance for professionals such as educators, rehabilitation personnel, employers and other persons who are substantially involved in the major life functions of the student.

As you can see, the definition of AT devices and services is very broad. Assistive technology services are not limited to evaluating the AT needs of students and providing AT devices. Assistive technology services include maintaining and customizing assistive technology devices and training students and others in how to use assistive technology devices. It is important to note that assistive technology devices and services may be provided for the student's use at home or in other settings. Access to assistive technology devices in the home or other settings is required if the IEP team decides the student needs access to the devices in order to receive an appropriate education.[29]

Extended School Year

For some students with disabilities, interrupting their school program for extended periods of time, such as during the summer break,

Assistive technology devices are items and pieces of equipment that are used to increase, maintain, or improve functional capabilities of children with disabilities.

---

[28] 20 U.S.C. 1402(1) and (2)
[29] *OSEP Policy Letter to Anonymous*, 18 IDELR 627 (11/21/91)

jeopardizes the benefit they receive from that program during the regular school year. These students need services during the summer to receive a free appropriate public education. Services provided in the summer are called extended school year services or ESY services. Extended school year services are special education and related services that are provided to a child with a disability beyond the normal school year of the school district.

The first court cases requiring extended school year services involved students with disabilities who, during the summer, lost skills they had learned during the previous school year. As a result of this loss of skills during the summer, the students were unable to benefit from their school program. These cases established a regression/recoupment standard for establishing the need for extended school year. The student lost skills during the summer, or regressed, so significantly that the student could not reasonably make up, or recoup, that loss the following school year.[30]

The courts noted that all students regress some during extended absences from school. Most students can make up that loss, in a reasonable amount of time, when they return to school. If it takes a student with a disability significantly longer to make up the loss, that student may be entitled to extended school year services. Thus, students who regressed significantly were entitled to services during the summer as part of receiving a free appropriate education.

Later court decisions allowed students to receive extended school year services without first being out of school during the summer months. If the IEP team could predict that the student was likely to regress, extended school year services could be included on the IEP.

Planning teams could look at how the student performed after being out of school during holidays or illnesses. Based on how the student performed upon returning to school, the IEP team could predict whether the student would be eligible for extended school year.

More recent court cases include factors, other than just regression/recoupment, in determining extended school year eligibility. The Tenth Circuit Court of Appeals, in *Johnson v. Independent School District No. 4*, included factors such as

- the degree of the student's impairment

- the ability of the student's parents to provide educational structure at home

- the student's rate of progress

- the student's behavioral and physical problems

- the availability of alternative resources

- the ability of the student to interact with students without disabilities

- the areas of the student's curriculum which need continuous attention

- the student's vocational needs

The Court in *Johnson* also looked at whether the service being requested for extended school year was extraordinary to this particular student or was an integral part of a program for students with this disability. If the service was an

---

30 *Battle v. Pennsylvania*, 629 F.2d 269 (3d Cir. 1980) *cert. denied*, 452 U.S. 968(1981), *Alamo Heights Independent School District v. State Board of Education*, 790 F.2d 1153 (5th Cir. 1986)

integral part of the program for students with this disability, provision for the service during the summer months could be required.[31]

Extended school year services must be provided only if a student's IEP team determines, on an individual basis, that extended school year services are needed for the student to receive an appropriate education. The school district may not (1) limit extended school year services to students with particular categories of disability; or (2) unilaterally limit the type, amount, or duration of the extended school year services. Additionally, since extended school year services are part of the provision of a free appropriate public education, the services must be provided according to an IEP and at no cost to the student's parents.

Extended school year services are not intended to continue the progress the student made during the normal school year through the summer. Rather, extended school year services are required to prevent jeopardizing progress the student has already made during the normal school year. Parents who believe their child may need extended school year services should make sure this topic is discussed at the IEP meeting. If the student has not already been out of school for a summer, parents should make sure the student's teachers are tracking the student's performance after school holidays and absences. This information will be needed to predict future regression.

School Records and Confidentiality

Under the IDEA parents have a right to examine all records relating to their child.[32] There is another law, the Family Educational Rights and Privacy Act (FERPA), that protects the privacy of educational records.[33] The Family Educational Rights and Privacy Act protects the confidentiality of educational records for all students. Educational records means records that are directly related to the student and are maintained by the educational agency or by someone acting on behalf of the educational agency.[34]

Educational records, however, do not include records that are kept in the sole possession of the professional making the record and that are not accessible to or revealed to any other person.[35] This means that records that teachers, supervisors, administrative personnel and support staff create and keep in their sole possession to help them do their jobs are generally not considered to be a student's educational record.

School personnel may not share the records or provide information from a student's records to unauthorized people. Of course, parents have the right to review their child's educational records. Moreover, school districts must provide access to the records without unnecessary delay, in no case waiting more than 45 days after the parents ask to review the records.[36]

Additionally, parents may get a copy of the records if, without having copies, they are effec-

---

[31] *Johnson v. Independent School District No. 4,* 921 F.2d 1022, 1027 (10th Cir. 1990), *cert. denied* 111 S.Ct. 1685 (1991)
[32] 20 U.S.C. 1415(b)(1)
[33] FERPA 20 U.S.C. 1232(g)
[34] FERPA Regulations 34 C.F.R. 99.3(a)
[35] FERPA Regulations 34 C.F.R. 99.3(b)
[36] FERPA 20 U.S.C. 1232(g) and 34 C.F.R. 99.10

The Family Educational Rights and Privacy Act protects the confidentiality of educational records for all students.

tively prevented from exercising their right to review and inspect the records. The district, however, may charge a fee for copies of the records, so long as the fee doesn't effectively prevent the parents from reviewing the records.[37] To protect the confidentiality of student records, schools must track who has looked at the records, when they looked, and why they looked.[38]

If parents believe that information contained in their child's records is inaccurate, misleading, or violates the child's privacy, the parents can ask the district to amend the information. If the district refuses to amend the student's record, the district must tell the parents they may appeal that decision. If the parents appeal, they have the right to a hearing regarding whether the information should be amended. If the hearing officer decides that the information doesn't have to be amended, the parents still have the right to include a statement in their child's records commenting on the questioned information and saying why the parents disagreed with it.[39]

Notes:

Again, the Family Educational Rights and Privacy Act (FERPA) protects the privacy rights of **all** students--students with and without disabilities. Generally, FERPA gives these privacy rights to parents to exercise on behalf of their children. The privacy rights under FERPA transfer to the student at the age of 18, or when the student attends a school beyond the high school level. Students who are 18 or attending school beyond the high school level are called **eligible students**.[40]

The Family Educational Rights and Privacy Act is enforced by the Family Policy Compliance Office within the United States Department of Education. Parents or eligible students may file complaints with that office. Complaints must contain specific allegations of fact that will give reasonable cause that FERPA has been violated. For more information regarding FERPA, please see the United States Department of Education website at http://www.ed.gov/policy/gen/guid/fpco/ferpa/index.html.

---

[37] FERPA Regulations 34 C.F.R. 99.10 to 99.12
[38] FERPA Regulations 34 C.F.R. 99.32
[39] FERPA Regulations 34 C.F.R. 99.20 to 99.22
[40] FERPA Regulations 34 C.F.R. 99.3

Notes:

II Least Restrictive Environment

Least restrictive environment. Three words stating a simple idea. The idea? Schools should keep kids in regular classes, and neighborhood students should attend neighborhood schools. Least restrictive environment, or LRE, charges schools to integrate students with disabilities with students without disabilities. Least restrictive environment permeates throughout the IDEA and Section 504 of the Rehabilitation Act. Later, we'll discuss least restrictive environment and Section 504; here we'll focus on LRE and the IDEA.

There are two elements to least restrictive environment: Classroom integration and neighborhood placement. Schools should educate students with disabilities, to the maximum extent appropriate, with students without disabilities. Before schools place students with disabilities in special classes, separate schools, or otherwise remove students from the regular educational environment, schools must consider using supplementary aids and services to help the student succeed in the regular classroom.[41]

As you know, supplementary aids and services are things we can provide to keep kids in regular classrooms. Before IEP teams place a student with a disability in a more restrictive setting than the regular classroom, they must consider using supplementary aids and services to help the regular classroom placement succeed. The IEP team should always try its best to keep kids with disabilities in regular classrooms.

Additionally, unless the student's IEP requires otherwise, the student should attend the school she would attend if she did not have a disability. Thus, if possible, students with disabilities attend their neighborhood school.

---

[41] 20 U.S.C. 1412(a)(5)

We try, through the IEP process, to make sure that students with disabilities go to school with their brothers, sisters, and other children in the neighborhood. This is not an absolute. If a student is unable, for valid educational reasons, to attend her neighborhood school, she should attend a school as close to home as possible.

The IEP team arrives at the least restrictive environment, step by step. The team begins by assuming the student will attend a regular classroom in her neighborhood school. If there are educational reasons why placement in the regular classroom might not be successful, the team considers providing supplementary aids and services to make the regular classroom placement succeed.

If, after considering using supplementary aids and services, the team finds the regular classroom placement won't work, it can look at the next, more restrictive, possible placement. In looking at the next possible setting, the team repeats the process. If that setting doesn't work, the team again considers using supplementary aids and services to make the placement succeed. Remember, the team arrives at the least restrictive environment, step by step.

You'll recall that supplementary aids and services are aids, services, and supports provided in regular education classes or other education-related settings that enable students with disabilities to be educated with students without disabilities to the maximum extent appropriate. Supplementary aids and services can include teacher training and support, itinerant instruction, modified curriculum, paraprofessional support, and assistive technology.

Always, the team must consider the feasibility of providing supplementary aids and services before the team removes the student from the regular classroom, placing her in a more restrictive setting. Again, the IEP team arrives at the least restrictive environment, step by step.

The Courts and LRE

When looking at a school district's determination of the least restrictive environment for a particular student, the courts have focused mostly on the process or steps the IEP team uses to arrive at the least restrictive environment. In 2004 in *L.B. and J.B. v. Nebo School District*, the 10th Circuit Court of Appeals reviewed the IDEA's least restrictive environment mandate.[42] At the outset, the Court noted the importance Congress placed on the least restrictive environment requirement:

"In enacting the IDEA, Congress explicitly mandated through the least restrictive environment requirement, that disabled children be educated in regular classrooms to the maximum extent appropriate. The LRE mandate provides that 'removal of children with disabilities from the regular educational environment occur only when the nature or severity of the disability of the child is such that education in regular classes with the use of supplementary aids and services cannot be achieved satisfactorily.' Educating children in the least restrictive environment

> The IEP team arrives at the least restrictive environment, step by step. The team begins by assuming the student will attend a regular classroom in her neighborhood school.

[42] *L.B. and J.B. v. Nebo School District*, 379 F3d. 966 (10th Cir. 2004)

in which they can receive a free appropriate public education is one of the IDEA's most important substantive requirements. Thus, the LRE requirement is a **specific statutory mandate. It is not. . .a question about educational methodology.** "[43]

The Court then established a process for determining least restrictive environment. The Court first looked at whether the education for the student in the regular classroom with the use of supplementary aids and services could be achieved satisfactorily. To make that determination the Court considered

1. the steps the school district has taken to accommodate the child in the regular classroom, including considering the continuum of placement and support services;

2. comparing the academic benefits the child receives in the regular classroom with the benefits the child will receive in the special education classroom;

3. the child's overall educational experience in regular education, including nonacademic benefits; and

4. the effect on the regular classroom of the presence of the child with a disability.[44]

If, after considering these factors, the Court determines that the student cannot be educated successfully in the regular classroom, it then looks to see if the school district has mainstreamed the student to the maximum extent appropriate. That is, if the student cannot be educated successfully in the regular classroom, the placement discussion is not over. The school district must still consider these factors in discussing placing the student in the next more-restrictive-placement on the continuum.

In adopting the above standard for determining the least restrictive environment, the 10th Circuit chose a standard previously adopted by the Third and Fifth Circuit Courts of Appeal.[45] This LRE standard is often referred to as the *Daniel R.R.* standard based on the 1989 Fifth Circuit case of *Daniel R.R. v. Board of Education*.[46] Moreover, the Tenth Circuit specifically decided not to use the *Roncker* standard adopted by the Fourth, Sixth, and Eighth Circuits.

The case of *Roncker v. Walter* was a 1983 Sixth Circuit case that said "[in] a case where the segregated facility is considered superior, the court should determine whether the services which make that placement superior could be feasibly provided in a non-segregated setting. If they can, the placement in the segregated school would be appropriate under the Act."[47] The Tenth Circuit decided not to use the *Roncker* test because that test is only useful in cases in which the more restrictive placement is considered a better educational choice and is not helpful in cases, such as *Nebo*, where the more integrated setting is considered educationally better.[48]

If a special education case is in due process or in litigation (see Chapter V on **Resolving Disputes Under the IDEA**), it is important to look at which

---

[43] *Nebo* at 976 emphasis supplied and internal citations omitted.

[44] *Nebo* at 977 to 979

[45] *Nebo* at 976 10th Circuit refers to the *Daniel R.R.* standard adopted by the 5th Circuit in *Daniel R.R. v. Bd. of Education*, 874 F.2d. 1036, 1048 (5th Cir.1989) and by the 3rd Circuit in *Oberti v. Bd. of Education*, 995 F.2d. 1204 (3rd Cir.1993)

[46] *Daniel R.R. v Bd. of Education*, 874 F.2d. 1048 (5th Circuit 1989)

[47] *Roncker v. Walter*, 700 F.2d. 1058 at 1063 (6th Cir.1983)

[48] *Nebo* at 978

Circuit Court of Appeals has jurisdiction over the federal courts in your state to determine how a federal court in your state will analyze least restrictive environment or other educational issues.[49] But from an educational perspective, IEP teams rarely spend time discussing court cases and judicial determinations. This is as it should be. The IEP team should focus on the needs of the student and the design of a program to meet those needs, not on a debate of legal issues. In that context, the 10th Circuit's discussion in *Nebo* is very helpful. *Nebo* is a judicial decision, but it outlines a clear process an IEP team can use to arrive at the least restrictive environment for a particular student.

First, the IEP team looks at whether the student's placement in the regular classroom can be achieved satisfactorily. To make that determination, the team must consider providing supplementary aids and services to support a successful classroom placement. The IEP team should consider several factors in deciding whether the student's classroom placement in the regular classroom, with the use of supplementary aids and services, can be achieved satisfactorily. Those factors are as follows:

- Consider steps to accommodate the student and consider a continuum of placement and support services.

- Compare the academic benefits of the regular classroom with the benefits of the more special education classroom.

- Discuss the student's overall experience in regular education including **nonacademic benefits**.

- Consider the effect of the student's presence on the regular classroom.

Second, if after considering the above steps, the IEP team determines that educating this student in the regular classroom cannot be achieved satisfactorily, the team still tries to mainstream the student to the maximum extent appropriate. Thus, the team should go through the same process in considering more restrictive educational settings.

Supplementary Aids and Services

In the course of reviewing the least restrictive environment requirement, the courts have required school districts to consider providing a range of supplementary aids and services before removing students from regular classrooms. Among those supplementary aids and services were the following:

- the assistance of an itinerant instructor with special education training

- special education training for the regular teacher

- modification of some of the academic curriculum to accommodate the student's disabilities

- parallel instruction to allow him to learn at his academic level

- provision of a part-time aide or paraprofessional

- use of a resource room[50]

---

[49] See Appendix E for a listing of the federal circuit courts of appeal and which states each court covers.

[50] *Oberti v. Board of Education*, 995 F.2d 1204 at 1222 (3rd Cir. 1993) also see *Greer v. Rome City School District*, 967 F.2d 470 (11th Cir. 1992) *Sacramento City Unified School District v. Rachel H.*, 14 F.2d 1398 at 1401 (9th Cir. 1994) *cert. denied*, 512 U.S. 1207 (1994)

LRE and the IEP

The IDEA's requirements for the individualized educational program (IEP) facilitate placing students in the least restrictive environment. The IEP must include statements explaining the extent to which the student will not participate with students without disabilities in the regular classroom and nonacademic and extra-curricular activities.[51] Similarly, the IEP must address how the student's disability affects her involvement in the general curriculum; it must state the specific supplementary aids and services and program modifications to be provided to the student.[52]

Moreover, the school district must ensure that the student with a disability participates in non-academic and extra curricular activities with students without disabilities to the maximum extent appropriate to the needs of the student with a disability. Examples of extra curricular and nonacademic activities include meals, recess periods, counseling services, athletics, transportation, health services, recreational activities, special interest groups or clubs sponsored by the school district, and referrals to agencies that provide assistance to individuals with disabilities.[53] Additionally, the school district must ensure that each child with a disability has the supplementary aids and services that the IEP team determined were needed for the student to participate in these nonacademic settings.[54]

A regular education teacher must be included as a member of the IEP team if the student is participating in the regular education environment or may be participating in the regular education environment.[55] The regular education teacher should participate in developing the student's IEP including determining "positive behavioral interventions and supports, and other strategies" and in choosing "supplementary aids and services, program modifications, and supports for school personnel. . ."[56]

Thus, the regular education teacher helps decide the supports needed for the student to succeed in the regular classroom in general, and in her classroom in particular. The regular education teacher has input into what can help the student to be successful and what can help the regular education teacher help the student. Participating in the meeting, first hand, is likely to help the regular education teacher understand why the student needs particular services, modifications, or accommodations and how to provide those supports. The teacher will have the opportunity to ask questions and tell the team what support the teacher may need to ensure the student is successful in the regular education classroom.

The IEP team must include "not less than one regular education teacher."[57] Sometimes it may be appropriate to include more than one regular education teacher as a member of the IEP team. This is particularly true for students who

> A regular education teacher must be included as a member of the IEP team if the student is participating in the regular education environment or may be participating in the regular education environment.

---

[51] 20 U.S.C. 1414(d)(1)(A)(IV)(bb) and (cc)
[52] 20 U.S.C. 1414(d)(1)(A)(I)(aa)(II)(aa)(IV)(bb)(cc)(V)(VI)
[53] 34 CFR 300.107(b) and 34 CFR 300.117
[54] 34 CFR 300.117
[55] 20 U.S.C. 1414(d)(1)(B)(ii)
[56] 20 U.S.C. 1414(d)(3)(C)
[57] 20 U.S.C. 1414(d)(1)(B)(ii)

are in middle school or high school and have more than one teacher. The IDEA allows the parents or school district to include "other individuals who have knowledge or special expertise regarding the child" as members of the team. So, parents may request that other regular education teachers attend the IEP meeting to learn about the student and contribute to developing the student's IEP.

To be sure, the more individuals that are included on the IEP team, the more difficult it may be to coordinate scheduling the IEP meeting. Parents may need to be extra patient in getting the meeting scheduled if the parents are requesting an additional regular education teacher or teachers attend. As we will discuss in Chapter IV, the IDEA 2004 encourages "alternative means of meeting participation."[58]

For example, the parents and the school district may agree to participation using telephone conference calls and video conferences.

The IDEA 2004 also allows some flexibility in team member attendance. If parents and the school district agree, a team member may be excused from attending portions of the meeting if "the member's area of the curriculum or related services is not being modified or discussed in the meeting."[59] This flexibility and the practice of using alternative means of participating in the IEP meeting may help regular education teachers and others participate in the meeting. By including regular education teachers in the IEP process, the IDEA has strengthened the process to fully include students with disabilities in the schools. Fully including students with disabilities is what least restrictive environment is all about.

Notes:

---

[58] 20 U.S.C. 1414(f)
[59] 20 U.S.C. 1414(d)(1)(c)(i)

III Evaluating the Needs of Students with Disabilities

Before children are placed in special education, they must be evaluated to determine whether they have a disability that requires special education services. If so, they are eligible for services under the IDEA. The evaluation process will also determine a particular child's specific educational needs. The IEP team conducts the evaluation process. A discussion of the three different types of evaluation follow.

The first evaluation is to determine whether the child has a disability that requires special education services. This is often referred to as the **initial evaluation**. After the initial evaluation the student must be **re-evaluated** at least every three years or whenever conditions warrant a re-evaluation, or whenever the student's teachers or parents request a re-evaluation. A student must also be re-evaluated if a change in the student's educational placement is contemplated. Finally, parents have the right to obtain an **independent**

educational evaluation, at any time, from an agency or provider outside the school district. As we will see, in some circumstances, the school district may be required to pay for the independent educational evaluation.

Initial Evaluation

The first step in this process requires that children who have been referred for possible special education placement be assessed or tested. The State Education Agency and school districts have an obligation to do *child find*. Child find means that all children with disabilities in the state (including homeless children, children who are wards of the state, and children in private schools) who may need special education and related services are identified, located, and evaluated.[60]

---

[60] 20 U.S.C. 1412(a)(3)

Once the assessments are completed, the results will be discussed by the IEP team to determine the child's eligibility for special education services. If the child is eligible for services, the team will complete the IEP. The IDEA has very specific safeguards regarding how children are to be evaluated. These safeguards are included to make sure that children are not misidentified as having disabilities, misclassified, or are placed inappropriately.

Referral for Initial Evaluation

Before a student can receive special education services under the IDEA, the student must have a full and individual initial evaluation.[61] Parents, the State Education Agency, the school district, or other state agencies may begin a request for an initial evaluation to determine if a child has a disability.[62] Thus, if parents are concerned that their child has a disability and may need special education services, parents may contact their school district and request that the child be evaluated.

In most cases school districts evaluate children to determine whether they need special education services if requested to do so. Technically, however, the IDEA does not mandate that school districts test all students for whom they receive requests for evaluations.[63] For example, if a district strongly believes it has no basis for suspecting a student has a disability, the district might decline to test the student. But if the school district refuses a parent's request to evaluate their child, the district must explain to the parents why the district is refusing to conduct the evaluation.

Moreover, the school district must tell the parents that the parents have a right to request a due process hearing to challenge the district's

refusal to evaluate. As we will discuss in Chapter V, due process hearings are usually costly for all involved. Thus, as a practical matter, school districts will likely conduct an initial evaluation if a child is referred for an evaluation.

The IDEA 2004 requires that the initial evaluation must be completed within **60 days** of the school district receiving the parent's consent for evaluation. If the state has established a different time frame that is shorter, then the evaluation must be completed within that time frame.

The initial evaluation must determine the student's educational needs as well as the student's eligibility for special education.[64] It is important that the initial evaluation determine not just eligibility for services, but that it also identify the student's educational needs. Having the educational needs identified helps the IEP team to develop a plan to meet those needs.

> The initial evaluation must determine the student's educational needs as well as the student's eligibility for special education.

Consent

Before the school district can evaluate a child, the district must obtain the parents' written informed consent. Informed consent means that

---

[61] 20 U.S.C. 1414(a)(1)(A)
[62] 20 U.S.C. 1414(a)(1)(B)
[63] Note that while the IDEA may not mandate that all students be tested upon referral, individual states may require that students be tested if referred for testing. The reader should, therefore, check the requirements in their state.
[64] 20 U.S.C. 1414(a)(1)(C) Note that the 60-day timeline refers to days, not school days.

the parents have been told, in writing, that the district wants to evaluate the child and the district has described for the parents the proposed evaluation procedures.[65]

The parents' consent to having their child evaluated is **not** consent to having the child receive special education services.[66] Once the evaluation process is complete and, if the IEP team determines the student is eligible for special education services under the IDEA, the school district must again obtain the parents' informed consent to the student receiving special education services. If the parents refuse to consent to having their child evaluated for eligibility for special education services, the school district may request a due process hearing and ask an impartial hearing officer to order the evaluation of the child.[67]

Again, consent to evaluation is **not** consent to receiving special education services. If the student's parents refuse to consent to the student receiving services, the school district is specifically prohibited from using due process to override the parents' refusal to consent to services. In short, the school district may use a due process hearing to override a parent's refusal to consent to an initial evaluation for

Before the school district can evaluate a child, the district must obtain the parents' written informed consent. Informed consent means that the parents have been told, in writing, that the district wants to evaluate the child and the district has described for the parents the proposed evaluation procedures.

eligibility for special education services, but the school district may not use a due process hearing to override a parent's refusal to consent to the student actually receiving those services.

Screening

The IDEA 2004 specifically separates "the screening of a student by a teacher or specialist to determine appropriate instructional strategies for curriculum implementation" from the definition of an initial evaluation for eligibility for special education services.[68] Thus, the school district does not need to obtain the parents' informed consent for a teacher or specialist to screen a student to determine instructional strategies to implement a curriculum.

Evaluation Process

When evaluating students the school district must use a "variety of assessment tools and strategies to gather relevant functional, developmental, and academic information, **including information provided by the parent. . .**"[69] This variety of tools, strategies and information is used to help determine (1) whether the student has a disability and, if so, (2) the content of the student's individualized educational program.[70] School districts may not use any "single measure or assessment as the **sole criterion for determining whether** the student has a disability or for determining the student's educational program."[71] Thus, the stu-

---

[65] 20 U.S.C. 1414(a)(1)(D)(i)(I) See also the written prior notice requirements at 20 U.S.C. 1415(a)(3) and (c).
[66] 20 U.S.C. 1414(a)(D)(i)(II)
[67] 20 U.S.C. 1414(a)(1)(D)(ii)
[68] 20 U.S.C. 1414(a)(1)(E)
[69] 20 U.S.C. 1414(b)(2)(A) emphasis applied.
[70] 20 U.S.C. 1414(b)(2)(A)(i)(ii)
[71] 20 U.S.C. 1414(b)(2)(B) emphasis applied.

dent cannot be identified as a student with a disability or the student's IEP developed based only on one assessment or measure.

The IDEA 2004 requires that assessments of children with disabilities are individualized and that the testing instruments are not racially or culturally biased.[72] To that end, tests and other evaluation materials must be "provided and administered in the language and form most likely to yield accurate information on what the child knows and can do academically, developmentally, and functionally unless it is not feasible. . ."[73] This means that if a child uses sign language or communicates through an augmentative communication device, the evaluations should be done with a sign language interpreter or with the child having access to the communication device.

Additionally, the tests must be administered by trained and knowledgeable people, must be used for purposes for which they are valid and reliable, and must be administered according to the instructions provided by the producer of the assessment.[74]

The evaluation process is multi-disciplinary. This means the child will be assessed by a team of individuals, each member of the team coming from a different discipline or area of expertise. Children must be assessed in all areas in which it is anticipated that they may have a disability. The evaluators must also use a variety of assessment tools and strategies to gather information to develop the child's IEP. Information provided from the child's parents should be included in the evaluation process. As discussed in the previous chapter regarding least restrictive environment, information that focuses on helping the child to be involved in the general education curriculum should also be considered.[75]

Again, no one procedure can be used as the sole basis for determining whether a child has a disability or for determining the child's educational program. Remember, the school district must notify parents that their child is going to be evaluated and describe the evaluation procedures that will be used. Parents must give their written permission for the evaluation to take place.

You may recall that assistive technology evaluations are included in the definition of assistive technology services. An assistive technology evaluation includes a functional evaluation of the child. A functional evaluation focuses on how assistive technology can help a child perform a task, such as writing, rather than focusing on why the child cannot perform the task. This evaluation must be conducted in the child's customary environment.[76] The child's customary environment is a place the child is used to, or comfortable in, such as the child's home or classroom.

Once evaluations have been completed, the assessment information is reviewed by the IEP

> The evaluation process is multi-disciplinary. This means the child will be assessed by a team of individuals, each member of the team coming from a different discipline or area of expertise.

[72] 20 U.S.C. 1414(b)(3)(A)

[73] 20 U.S.C. 1414(b)(3)(ii) It should be noted that previously, under the IDEA 97, tests and assessments had to be administered in the child's "native language."

[74] 20 U.S.C. 1414(b)(3)(iii)(iv)(v)

[75] 20 U.S.C. 1414(b)(2)(ii)

[76] 20 U.S.C. 1402(2)

team. The child's parents are members of the IEP team.[77] Parents, therefore, have an opportunity to review existing evaluation information about their child and to request additional information regarding specific areas, such as assistive technology, that may be needed to develop the child's program. If parents believe their child may have needs that are not being addressed, the parents should specifically request an assessment of the child in that particular area.

Specific Learning Disabilities

There is an important change in the IDEA 2004 regarding local school districts using the severe discrepancy standard to determine whether a student has a specific learning disability. The definition of specific learning disability has not changed. "Specific learning disability means a disorder in 1 or more of the basic psychological processes involved in understanding or in using language, spoken or written, which disorder may manifest itself in the imperfect ability to listen, think, speak, read, write, spell, or do mathematical calculations."[78] Under the regulations implementing the IDEA 97, IEP teams could identify a student as having a learning disability if the student had a severe discrepancy between achievement and intellectual ability in certain areas. Now, under the IDEA 2004, school districts cannot be required to use the severe discrepancy

> Now, under the IDEA 2004, school districts cannot be required to use the severe discrepancy standard when determining whether a student has a specific learning disability.

standard when determining whether a student has a specific learning disability.[79]

Severe Discrepancy Standard

The severe discrepancy standard looks at whether a student's classroom achievement matches the student's age and ability levels in certain areas like oral expression, written expression, reading skill, mathematical reasoning and mathematical calculation. Under the regulations implementing the IDEA 97, the U.S. Department of Education established a severe discrepancy formula as part of the criteria for determining that a student has a specific learning disability.

According to the IDEA 97 regulations, the IEP team could determine that a student had a specific learning disability if the team: (1) determined that the student was not achieving commensurate (equal) with the student's age and ability in one or more areas like oral expression, listening comprehension, written expression, basic reading skill, reading comprehension, mathematics calculation, or mathematics reasoning; and then determined (2) that the student has a severe discrepancy (inconsistency) between achievement and intellectual ability in one or more of the areas just mentioned.[80]

---

[77] 20 U.S.C. 1414(1)(d)(B)(i)
[78] 20 U.S.C. 1402(30)(A) Note the term learning disability includes conditions such as "perceptual disabilities, brain injury, minimal brain dysfunction, dyslexia, and developmental aphasia." 20 U.S.C. 1402(30)(B) But the "term does not include a learning problem that is primarily the result of visual, hearing, or motor disabilities, of mental retardation, of emotional disturbance, or of environmental, cultural, or economic disadvantage." 20 U.S.C. 1402(30)(C)
[79] 20 U.S.C. 1414(b)(6)(A)
[80] 34 C.F.R. 300.541

In reauthorizing the IDEA 2004, however, Congress was concerned that the severe discrepancy approach could not be applied "in a consistent (i.e., reliable and valid) manner." Moreover, Congress was concerned that the severe discrepancy approach was "problematic for students living in poverty or with or from culturally and linguistically different backgrounds" because these students may be mistakenly viewed as having learning disabilities when their difficulty on these intellectual tests are really because of their lack of experience or educational opportunity.[81]

Thus, under the IDEA 2004, State Education Agencies cannot require local school districts in their state to consider whether the student "has a severe discrepancy between achievement and intellectual ability in oral expression, listening, comprehension, written expression, basic reading skill, reading comprehension, mathematical calculation, or mathematical reasoning."[82] Moreover state education agencies must adopt criteria for determining whether a student has a specific learning disability. Those criteria cannot require the use of the severe discrepancy standard and must permit the use of "a process based on the child's response to scientific, research based intervention..."[83] The state criteria

for determining whether a student has a specific learning disability *may* permit using other research based procedures for determining whether a student has a learning disability.[84]

As noted, the IDEA 2004 specifically allows school districts to use a response to intervention process to determine whether a student has a learning disability. A response to intervention (RTI) process is a process that determines how the student "responds to scientific, research-based intervention..." as part of the evaluation process.[85]

Under the response to intervention process, before identifying the student as having a learning disability and placing the student in special education, educators look at how the student is performing in the general curriculum. If there are questions regarding how the student is performing, teachers try "interventions" to improve the student's performance. Some examples of interventions are more specialized teaching staff, smaller teacher-student ratios, more time in the subject, and more intense programs.[86]

After educational interventions are tried, data is collected to assess how well the intervention worked. If the student's performance doesn't satisfactorily improve, then the student may be determined to have a specific learning disability. In some models, several layers or tiers of interventions may be used. Each tier provides a more intense intervention.[87] Under the IDEA 2004 the "interventions" must be "scientific, research-based" interventions.

Note that the IDEA 2004 does not prohibit a school district from using a severe discrepancy standard; it just says the district cannot be required to use it. Likewise, the IDEA 2004 doesn't require a school district to use a

[81] S.Rept. 185, 108th Cong., 2d Sess. 26 (2003)

[82] 20 U.S.C. 1414(b)(6)(A)

[83] 34 CFR 300.307(a)(1) and (2)

[84] 34 CFR 300.307(a)(3)

[85] 20 U.S.C. 1414(b)(6)(B) see also *Q and A: Questions and Answers On Response to Intervention (RTI) and Early Intervening Services (EIS)* http://idea.ed.gov (OSERS 2007).

[86] *A Parents Guide to Response-to-Intervention,* page 3, http://www.ncld.org/images/stories/downloads/parent_center/rti_final.pdf. National Center for Learning Disabilities (2006)

[87] *A Parents Guide to Response-to-Intervention,* page 6, http://www.ncld.org/images/stories/downloads/parent_center/rti_final.pdf. National Center for Learning Disabilities (2006)

response to scientific intervention model, but it authorizes the use of a response to scientific intervention process.

Attention Deficit Disorder and Attention Deficit Hyperactivity Disorder

Although attention deficit disorder (ADD) and attention deficit hyperactivity disorder (ADHD) are not listed as a separate disability category in the IDEA, children with these disabilities **can be eligible** for IDEA services. Attention deficit disorder and attention deficit hyperactivity disorder can be included as a specific learning disability or in the category of other health impairments (OHI). Other health impairments can include a variety of impairments that are due to chronic or acute health problems. Included as other health impairments are asthma, attention deficit disorder or attention deficit hyperactivity disorder, diabetes, epilepsy, heart conditions, hemophilia, lead poisoning, leukemia, nephritis, rheumatic fever, and sickle cell anemia.[88]

Note that children with ADD or ADHD and other health impairments such as asthma, diabetes, epilepsy, leukemia, etc. can be eligible for IDEA services, **provided that the child needs special education and related services**. The IEP team will determine if the student needs special education and related services. Not all children with ADD or ADHD, or other health impairments, will need special education and related services because of those impairments. But if the impairment results in the need for special education and related services, the student is eligible for IDEA services. If the student with ADD, ADHD, or another health impairment is not eligible for IDEA services, the student may be eligible for services under

Section 504. Again, we'll specifically discuss Section 504 in Chapter VIII.

Sometimes children with ADD or ADHD and other conditions are treated with medication. In the past there has been some concern that children might be unnecessarily medicated and that schools have sometimes required children to be on medication in order to attend school. The IDEA 2004 specifically requires that each State Education Agency prohibit school personnel from requiring a child to obtain a prescription for a controlled substance in order to attend school, be evaluated, or receive special education services.[89]

Re-evaluation

Once a child with a disability has been evaluated and placed into special education, the evaluation process is not over. Children change as they grow, learn, and develop. A child's disabilities may change in their nature or severity. The IDEA, therefore, provides that children are re-evaluated if conditions warrant or if the child's teacher or parents request re-evaluation. A re-evaluation must be done at least every three years.[90] Additionally, a child with a disability must be evaluated before the child can be determined to no longer have a disability

> Once a child with a disability has been evaluated and placed into special education, the evaluation process is not over. Children change as they grow, learn, and develop.

---

[88] 34 C.F.R. 300.8(c)(9)
[89] 20 U.S.C. 1412(a)(25)
[90] 20 U.S.C. 1414(a)(2)(A)(B)

and, therefore, no longer be eligible for services under the IDEA.[91]

Some students with disabilities may graduate from school and receive a regular education diploma. Others may stay in school and receive special education services until they reach the age of twenty-one and are no longer eligible for services age-wise. School districts are not required to re-evaluate the student if the student's eligibility for services is ending because the student is graduating with a regular diploma or the student is no longer eligible age-wise for services.[92]

When conducting an initial or re-evaluation, the IEP team will review all the existing evaluation data on the student. The team will look at evaluations and information from the student's parents, classroom-based observations, and observations by teachers and related service providers. The team will also look at current classroom-based assessments, including local or state assessments.[93] Basing its decision on a review of the information, the team will determine the student's present levels of academic achievement and developmental needs. The team will also determine

- whether the student has a disability;

- whether the student needs special education and related services;

- whether any additions, or modifications are needed to help the student meet the annual measurable goals in the student's IEP; and

- whether any additions or modifications are needed to help the student participate in the general curriculum.[94]

The IEP team will consider whether new assessments are needed to determine any of the above information. If the team believes more assessments and evaluations are needed, the school district will make sure the additional assessments are done.[95] If the IEP team decides that additional assessments are needed, the school district is required to get the parents' informed consent to those assessments. However, if the school district makes a reasonable effort to get consent and the parents don't respond, it may be excused from obtaining consent.[96] On the other hand, the IEP team may determine that it does not need any additional data to complete the re-evaluation. If so, the team tells the student's parents that the team believes no new data is needed. But if the parents disagree and request additional assessments, then the additional assessments must be conducted.[97]

The IDEA specifically allows the IEP team, in the re-evaluation process, to forgo retesting the student if no new testing is needed. The student, therefore, does not have to undergo additional testing if there is enough existing information to determine the child's eligibility for special education services and educational needs. This conserves resources and prevents students from being retested just for the sake of retesting. But remember, the student's parents have the right to have the student retested if they feel new assessments are needed.

Summary of Performance

The IDEA 2004 includes a new requirement that the school district provide students who are no longer eligible for IDEA services with a summary

---

[91] 20 U.S.C. 1414(a)(5)(A)
[92] 20 U.S.C. 1414(a)(5)(B)
[93] 20 U.S.C. 1414(c)(1)(A)
[94] 20 U.S.C. 1414(c)(1)(B)
[95] 20 U.S.C. 1414(c)(2)
[96] 20 U.S.C. 1414(c)(3)
[97] 20 U.S.C. 1414(c)(4)

of the student's academic achievement and functional performance. This summary must include recommendations on how to assist the student in meeting the student's postsecondary goals.[98] A summary that includes good documentation of the student's disability and needs, as well as of supports and accommodations the student needs to be successful, would be a very useful transition tool. A summary with that information could be used to document that the adult student is a person with a disability under Section 504 and the Americans with Disabilities Act.

Unlike the public schools, colleges and other post secondary institutions usually are not required to do assessments to determine if an individual has a disability and may need accommodations. Generally, in the postsecondary world, the individual is expected to provide documentation of disability and suggest accommodations needed. A well-written summary of performance might, therefore, be very useful to the student. This summary might also provide documentation that would help the adult student receive services from vocational rehabilitation services and other state and local disability service providers. Please note that state vocational rehabilitation

agencies (VR) are required to assess individuals seeking vocational rehabilitation services.

Independent Educational Evaluations

Parents have the right to obtain an independent educational evaluation of their child.[99] If parents disagree with the evaluations done by the school district, the parents may obtain an evaluation from an entity outside the school district. The parents might disagree with the results or the appropriateness of the school's evaluation. If parents obtain an independent evaluation, at their own expense, the IEP team is required to consider the results of that evaluation. Parents may also request that the school district pay the cost of the outside evaluation.

If parents request an independent evaluation, the school district must give the parents information about where the parents can get an independent evaluation and what criteria the district has regarding independent evaluations. If parents request an independent evaluation at the district's expense, it is the district's responsibility to either provide the evaluation, or schedule an administrative hearing to determine if the district's assessments were sufficient and accurate.

The administrative hearing, as discussed in Chapter V, is conducted by an impartial hearing officer. If the hearing officer determines the district's assessments were inappropriate, the district must pay the costs of the independent evaluation. On the other hand, should the hearing officer determine the district's assessments were accurate and sufficient, the parents would bear the costs of the independent evaluation.

> The IDEA 2004 includes a new requirement that the school district provide students who are no longer eligible for IDEA services with a summary of the student's academic achievement and functional performance. This summary must include recommendations on how to assist the student in meeting the student's postsecondary goals.

---

[98] 20 U.S.C. 1414(a)(5)(B)(ii)
[99] 20 U.S.C. 1415(b)(1)

Sometimes school districts will purchase independent evaluations to obtain additional information on a child's educational needs. The IEP team may welcome an independent assessment to help them meet a child's needs. Additionally, an independent evaluation can sometimes be useful to help resolve disagreements between a child's parents and school personnel. The opinion of an independent person, with "no axe to grind," may help the parents and the school resolve a disagreement and avoid the need to resort to lengthier dispute resolution procedures. An independent evaluation may be a very helpful tool for an IEP team to identify the needs of a student with a disability.

Notes:

IV

The Individualized Educational Program

All of the issues we have discussed thus far come together in the Individualized Educational Program or IEP. The IEP is the process and the document that outlines what a free appropriate public education is for a particular child. As we have seen, the IEP determines what the least restrictive environment is for an individual student and what supplementary aids and services the student may need to participate fully in the regular education environment. The IEP identifies the related services a child needs to benefit from his special education program. The IEP meeting is where the educational needs of students are discussed and identified. Fittingly, with the 2004 amendments to the IDEA, the IEP focuses more now than in the past on ensuring that students with disabilities have significant access to the general curriculum. In the IDEA 2004, Congress also encourages flexibility in the IEP process.

The IDEA 2004, for the first time, includes procedures to permit members of the IEP team to be excused from attending an IEP meeting if the team member's area of expertise or focus is not being addressed.[100] Also for the first time, the IDEA includes a process to allow the IEP to be amended without pulling together a meeting of all of the members of the team.[101]

> The IDEA 2004, for the first time, includes procedures to permit members of the IEP team to be excused from attending an IEP meeting if the team member's area of expertise or focus is not being addressed. Also for the first time, the IDEA includes a process to allow the IEP to be amended without pulling together a meeting of all of the members of the team.

[100] 20 U.S.C. 1414(d)(1)(C)
[101] 20 U.S.C. 1414(d)(3)(D)

The procedures for amending the IEP and excusing a team member from attending an IEP meeting, or part of an IEP meeting, will be discussed more fully later in this chapter. But it is important to note at the outset that the IEP cannot be amended, nor can a team member be excused from attending the meeting, unless both the student's parents and the school district agree and the parents consent in writing.

An appropriate educational program for each student with a disability is our destination. The IEP process is the vehicle that will get us there. We must understand and use this process to obtain appropriate services for students with disabilities.

> ...the IEP cannot be amended, nor can a team member be excused from attending the meeting, unless both the student's parents and the school district agree and the parents consent in writing.

Who Are the Members of the IEP Team?

Individualized Educational Programs or IEPs are written documents that outline specific educational plans for each student with a disability. There are very specific requirements regarding the contents of an IEP and a specific listing of the membership of the team charged with developing the IEP.[102] An appropriate education is individualized, but it takes a team to get there. Members of that team are

1. the student's parents;

2. not less than one of the student's regular education teachers, if the student currently is, or may be, participating in regular education;

3. not less than one of the student's special education teachers or, where appropriate, someone else who provides special education services to the student;

4. a representative of the school district who is qualified to provide, or supervise providing, specially designed instruction to meet the unique needs of students with disabilities and who is knowledgeable about both the general curriculum and the availability of the district's resources;

5. an individual who can interpret how the information from evaluations can impact the child's instruction;

6. at the parents' or school district's discretion, other individuals who have knowledge or special expertise regarding the child, including related services personnel;

7. the student with a disability whenever appropriate;

8. the Part C service coordinator or other representatives of the Part C system if the student has received Part C early childhood services and if the parents request their presence to help with the "smooth transition of services" from Part C to Part B.[103]

Parents are specifically listed as members of the IEP team. To facilitate parent participation in

[102] 20 U.S.C. 1414(d)(1)(B)
[103] 20 U.S.C. 1414(d)(1)(D)

developing the IEP, the school district is required to notify parents of the meeting. This notice must be provided in a reasonable time before the meeting. The meeting must also be scheduled at a reasonably convenient time for the parents. Moreover, if the parents are deaf or non-English speaking, interpreters must be provided.[104]

There may be other persons who attend an IEP meeting. Parents have the right to be assisted at the meeting by an attorney or anyone else they choose to assist them. Other individuals who might be members of the team are persons who have special knowledge or expertise regarding the special educational needs of the student. These individuals may be related service providers; they may be individuals who have conducted independent evaluations of the student; or they might be other regular education teachers. Additionally, **attending** the IEP meeting does not necessarily mean an individual is physically present at the meeting. The IDEA 2004 encourages alternative means of participating in the meeting. For example, the parents and the school district may agree to allow participation by conference calls and video conferences.[105]

As noted in Chapter II discussing least restrictive environment, a key member of the IEP team is the student's regular education teacher. The regular education teacher can be an important source of information regarding the supports the student might need to participate effectively in the regular classroom. Moreover, by attending the IEP meeting, the regular education teacher can learn about the student, the student's disability, and what services, accommodations, and modifications the student may need to be successful. It might be very helpful for the regular education teacher to understand

how and why these services are provided. Teachers that understand why a service, support, or accommodation is necessary are more likely to provide the support effectively.

We also discussed in Chapter II that the IDEA requires not less than one regular education teacher attend the IEP meeting. As we discussed, there might be times when having more than one regular education teacher would be appropriate. For example, if the student is in middle school or high school, the student will probably have several regular education teachers for several different classes. The student's teachers from the other regular education classes might also benefit from attending the meeting and contributing to developing the IEP.

Again, the IDEA only requires that not less than one regular education teacher attend the IEP meeting. But, as noted above, other individuals may be included on the team at the discretion of the parents or school district. So, parents may request that other regular educa-

> The regular education teacher can be an important source of information regarding the supports the student might need to participate effectively in the regular classroom. Moreover, by attending the IEP meeting, the regular education teacher can learn about the student, the student's disability, and what services, accommodations, and modifications the student may need to be successful.

---

[104] 20 U.S.C. 1415(d)(2)
[105] 20 U.S.C. 1414(f)

tion teachers attend, if appropriate. Again, as noted in Chapter II, if parents are requesting additional team members, the parents may need to be a little extra patient and extra flexible with the amount of time it takes to schedule the meeting. It's likely that the more people who will be attending, the more difficult it will be to coordinate the meeting schedule.

Team Absences

There might be times when it isn't necessary for an individual who is usually included on the IEP team to attend an IEP meeting or part of the meeting. So, the IDEA 2004 includes a procedure to excuse a team member from attending. The IDEA 2004 discusses two different situations in which an IEP team member may be excused from attending all or part of an IEP meeting: (1) the team member's area of the curriculum or related services **will not** be discussed during the meeting; or (2) the team member's area of the curriculum or related services **will** be discussed.

First, there are times when a team member's area of the curriculum or related services will not be discussed or modified at a particular IEP meeting or portion of a meeting. There are also occasions in which the team member may have provided input related to the team member's area of responsibility or expertise in an earlier portion of the meeting and needs to be excused from the later portions of the meeting. Occasionally IEP meetings last for several hours. Sometimes the IEP may not be completed in one meeting. Additional meetings may be needed. A team member may have given their input in the first

meeting and may not be needed for the subsequent meetings. If that is the case, the parents and the school district can agree to excuse the team member from attending the meeting.

Note, both the parents and the school district must agree to excuse an IEP team member from attending an IEP meeting.[106] Moreover, the parent must specifically agree and consent in writing to excusing the team member from attending the IEP meeting.[107]

Second, there also might be times when, even though a team member's area of curriculum or related services will be discussed at the meeting, it is helpful to excuse the team member from attending all, or part, of the IEP meeting. For example, an IEP meeting is needed, but a particular team member's schedule complicates arranging the meeting. In this case, the IDEA 2004 allows that if the parents and the school district agree, a team member may be excused from attending the meeting. In this example, however, since the team member's area of curriculum or related services **will** be discussed or modified at the meeting, the excused team member **must** submit input into developing the IEP **prior** to the meeting in **writing** to the **parent** and the IEP team.[108]

Again, a team member cannot be excused from attending an IEP meeting without the parent's written agreement and consent. Under this new provision allowing team absences, situations may arise in which parents have consented to excusing a team member from attending an IEP meeting, but during the meeting, the parents realize that they need the team member present. In that situation, perhaps the IEP meeting could be continued to another date or another IEP meeting could be scheduled to include the absent team member.

[106] 20 U.S.C. 1414(d)(1)(C)
[107] 20 U.S.C. 1414(d)(1)(C)(iii)
[108] 20 U.S.C. 1414(d)(1)(C)(ii)

What Are the Components of the IEP?

The IDEA is very specific regarding what an IEP must contain.[109] As we discussed in Chapter I, the 1997 amendments to the IDEA brought an increased emphasis on providing students with disabilities meaningful access to the general curriculum. The IDEA 2004 continues that emphasis. Thus, the IEP continues to focus on involving the student in the general curriculum and ensuring the student's progress in the general curriculum.

A proper IEP must include the following information. Please note that this language is not the exact language used in the IDEA. I have paraphrased to a certain extent to help make the legal language more understandable. I have also, in most places, used the word student in place of the word "child." The components of the IEP are described below:

1. A statement of the student's present levels of academic achievement and functional performance, including

   a. how the student's disability affects the student's involvement and progress in the general curriculum;

   b. for preschool children, as appropriate, how the disability affects the child's participation in appropriate activities; and

   c. for students who take alternate assessments aligned to alternate achievment standards, a description of benchmarks or short-term objectives.

2. A statement of measurable annual goals, including academic and functional goals, designed to

   a. meet the student's needs that result from the student's disability in a way that will enable the student to be involved in and make progress in the general curriculum; and

   b. meet the student's other educational needs that result from the student's disability.[110]

3. A statement about how the student's progress toward meeting the annual goals will be measured and when periodic reports on the progress the student is making toward meeting the annual goals will be provided (for example, using quarterly or other periodic reports, sent out at the same time report cards are issued).

4. A statement of the special education and related services and supplementary aids and services, *based on peer reviewed research to the extent practicable* to be provided to the student, or on behalf of the student. This must also include a statement of the program modifications or supports for school personnel that will be provided for the student[111]

> ...the IEP continues to focus on involving the student in the general curriculum and ensuring the student's progress in the general curriculum.

[109] 20 U.S.C. 1414(d)(1)(A)(aa)(bb)
[110] 20 U.S.C. 1414(d)(1)(A)(II) Note that the annual goals no longer need to include bench-marks and short-term objectives.
[111] 20 U.S.C. 1414(d)(1)(A)(IV) Note that the language in italics is new.

    a. to advance appropriately toward attaining the annual goals;

    b. to be involved and make progress in the general education curriculum and to make progress in extracurricular activities and other nonacademic activities; and

    c. to be educated and participate with other students with disabilities and students without disabilities in the general curriculum and extracurricular and other nonacademic activities.

5. An explanation of the extent that the student will **not** participate with children without disabilities in the regular classroom, extracurricular and nonacademic activities and other general curriculum activities, if any.

6. A statement of any individual appropriate accommodations that are necessary to measure academic achievement and functional performance on state and district-wide assessments, and if the IEP team determines the student shall take an alternate assessment on a state or district-wide assessment there must be

    a. a statement why the student cannot participate in the regular assessment; and

    b. a statement that the particular alternate assessment selected for the student is appropriate.

7. The **projected date** for the beginning of the services and modifications listed in item 4 above and the **anticipated frequency, location, and duration of those services and modifications.**

8. Beginning not later than the first IEP to be in effect when the student is 16, and updated annually afterwards,

    a. appropriate measurable postsecondary goals based on age appropriate transition assessments related to training, education, employment, and where appropriate, independent living schools;

    b. the transition services (including courses of study) needed to assist the student in reaching those goals; and

    c. beginning not later than one year before the student reaches the age of majority under state law, a statement that the student has been informed of his rights under the IDEA that will transfer when he reaches the age of majority.

Developing the IEP and Special Factors

Generally, when developing the IEP, the IEP team must take into account the student's strengths, the parents' concerns for enhancing their child's education, the results of the initial evaluation or the student's most recent evaluation, and the student's academic, developmental, and functional needs.[112]

There are also special factors that must be considered in developing the IEP.[113] If the student's behavior impedes the student's learning or the learning of other students, then positive behavioral interventions and supports and other strategies should be considered to address that

[112] 20 U.S.C. 1414(d)(3)(A)
[113] 20 U.S.C. 1414(d)(3)(B)

behavior. If the student has limited proficiency in English, the team should consider the student's language needs as they relate to the IEP.

Moreover, for students who are blind or have visual impairments the team should consider instruction in Braille unless the team feels that instruction in Braille would be inappropriate. The team should also consider the communication needs of the student. If the student is deaf or hard of hearing, the team should consider the student's language and communication needs, opportunities for direct communication with peers and professionals in the student's language and communication mode, academic level, and full range of needs, including opportunities for direct instruction in the student's communication and language mode.

This means that for students whose communication and language mode is American Sign Language, the team should consider providing opportunities for those students to communicate directly with other students and instructors who use American Sign Language, rather than through a sign language interpreter. Finally, included among those special factors is a requirement that the IEP team specifically consider whether the student requires assistive technology devices and services.

As you can see, the IDEA's requirements regarding the contents of the IEP are very

> ...the IDEA's requirements regarding the contents of the IEP are very prescriptive. This is important because developing the IEP is the key to delivering quality services to students with disabilities.

prescriptive. This is important because developing the IEP is the key to delivering quality services to students with disabilities. Once all the assessment data have been collected, the IEP meeting is where services for the student will be written into the IEP document. If the team is satisfied that sufficient data has been collected, then their next step is to ensure that the student's needs, with services to meet those needs, are written into the IEP.

Transfer Students

The IDEA 2004 clarifies the IEP process for students who transfer school districts during the school year. The IDEA 2004, first, provides the process for students who transfer school districts within the same state, and, second, discusses the process for students who transfer from outside the state.

Transfer Within the Same State

As we know, all students with disabilities are entitled to a free appropriate public education. So, if a student with an IEP transfers school districts within the state during the school year, the school district receiving the student must provide the student a free appropriate public education. That free appropriate public education will include services that are comparable or similar to the services described in the student's IEP from the previous school district. These comparable services in the new district must be developed in consultation with the student's parents. The **comparable** services will be provided until the receiving school district adopts the IEP from the previous school district or develops and implements a new IEP.[114]

---

[114] 20 U.S.C. 1414(d)(2)(C)(i)

Transfer from Outside the State

Similarly, if a student with an IEP transfers from a school district in one state to a school district in another state during the school year, the school district in the receiving state must provide the student a free appropriate public education. Also, that free appropriate public education will include services that are comparable to the services described in the student's IEP from the previous school district, and the services must be developed in consultation with the student's parents. These **comparable** services will be provided until the receiving school district, in the new state, evaluates the student, and if necessary, develops a new IEP.[115]

Transition Services

Transition services must be included on the first IEP that will be in effect at the time the student reaches the age of 16.[116] Transition services are a coordinated set of activities that facilitate moving the student from school to post-school activities smoothly. To that end, transition activities include post-secondary education, vocational training, integrated employment (including supported employment), continuing and adult education, adult services, independent living, or community participation.[117]

Since the transition plan is anticipating what the student will want to do in the student's post-school future, the transition plan must be based upon the individual student's needs and take into account the student's strengths, preferences and interests. Finally, the transition plan includes instruction, related services, community experiences, the development of employment and other post-school adult living objectives. Transition services can also include, when appropriate, acquiring daily living skills and functional vocational evaluation.[118]

In developing the transition portion of the IEP, the team must include "appropriate measurable postsecondary goals based upon age appropriate transition assessments related to training, education, employment, and where appropriate, independent living skills."[119] The transition activities must be designed within a "results-oriented process that is focused on improving the academic and functional achievement" of the student.[120] As noted above, the transition plan must take into account the student's preferences and interests. As part of determining those preferences and interests, it would be very appropriate to include the transitioning student in the IEP as a member of the IEP team.[121]

Transition services are a coordinated set of activities that facilitate moving the student from school to post-school activities smoothly. To that end, transition activities include post-secondary education, vocational training, integrated employment (including supported employment), continuing and adult education, adult services, independent living, or community participation.

---

[115] 20 U.S.C. 1414(d)(2)(C)(ii)
[116] 20 U.S.C. 1414(d)(1)(A)(VIII)(aa)(bb)
[117] 20 U.S.C. 1402(34)
[118] 20 U.S.C. 1402(34)
[119] 20 U.S.C. 1414(d)(1)(A)(VIII)(aa)
[120] 20 U.S.C. 1402(34)
[121] 20 U.S.C. 1414(d)(1)(B)(vii)

In coordinating the transition activities, the IEP team may want to include representatives or input from agencies such as the State Vocational Rehabilitation Agency (VR) and other agencies providing services to adults with disabilities. The State Vocational Rehabilitation Agency is required to provide services that are needed to help an individual with a disability obtain vocational goals and become employed.

Thus, to be eligible for vocational rehabilitation services, the student's disability must be a barrier to employment and the services must be needed to overcome that barrier. Since the Vocational Rehabilitation Agency is focused on overcoming barriers to employment, the VR Agency provides its services according to an Individualized Plan for Employment (IPE). While VR generally serves adults with disabilities, there is no age limitation for vocational rehabilitation services. Consequently, eligible students with disabilities can receive assistance from the Vocational Rehabilitation Agency at any age, depending upon their vocational needs.

Including the Vocational Rehabilitation Agency in the transition planning process can establish a link with VR while the student is still in school, as well as help identify supports the student will need after leaving school. Since both school districts and the Vocational Rehabilitation Agency have responsibilities to provide students with services, it might be important to include a statement on the student's IEP specifically clarifying what each agency will do and when they will do it. To facilitate developing these statements, the student's vocational rehabilitation counselor might be included in the IEP meeting.

Again, in developing a coordinated set of activities it might be useful to get input from agencies, other than the school district, that provide services to adults with disabilities. The transition process should include connecting the student, or providing linkages to people, organizations, and agencies the student may need to assist in transition or the student may need in the future. In making those connections, the **Summary of Performance** discussed in Chapter III, might be a very useful tool.

As noted earlier, the Summary of Performance is provided to the student by the school district if the student graduates with a regular diploma or when the student is no longer eligible for educational services because the student has reached the age of twenty-one. The Summary of Performance includes recommendations on how to assist the student in meeting postsecondary goals.[122] Those postsecondary goals should be stated on the IEP as part of the transition process.

Thus, the Summary of Performance could include, for example, recommendations regarding modifications, assistance, and accommodations the student may need from vocational schools, higher education, vocational rehabilitation, and adult disability service providers to meet the student's postsecondary goals.

Specific Services

The IEP team must include a statement of the special education and related services and supplementary aids and services that will be provided to the student as part of the IEP. Additionally, the IEP will include a statement of the program modifications or supports that will be provided for school staff to assist the student.[123]

---

[122] 20 U.S.C. 1414(c)(5)(B)(ii)
[123] 20 U.S.C. 1414(d)(1)(A)(IV)

> The IEP team must include a statement of the special education and related services and supplementary aids and services that will be provided to the student as part of the IEP.

Furthermore, once a service has been specifically written into the IEP, then the IEP must also include additional information to help ensure the services are provided. For each service and modification stated on the IEP, the IEP must also state

1. the projected date that service is to begin;

2. the anticipated frequency of the service;

3. the location where the service and modification will be provided; and

4. the duration, or how long, the service and modification will be provided.[124]

This information helps ensure that services are provided when and where they are meant to be delivered, for as long as the IEP team intended, and as often as the IEP team intended.

Reviewing, Revising, and Amending the IEP

Once the IEP process is completed and the IEP is written, it will remain in effect until the IEP team reviews and changes it, or the parents and the school district agree to amend it. The IEP must be reviewed at least annually, but it can be reviewed more frequently if necessary. The IEP

team can meet and review the IEP as necessary to address concerns as they arise.

For example, the student may not make the progress that was expected toward the annual goals. Perhaps the student has been re-evaluated and the team needs to meet to discuss the results of the re-evaluation. Or, maybe the student's parents have new information regarding the student that needs to be considered by the IEP team.[125] Thus, when necessary, the IEP team can meet to review and revise the IEP. Sometimes the parents and school district may want to change the IEP, but they may not feel that it is necessary to convene an IEP meeting to make the changes. The IDEA 2004 has a new process to amend the IEP without convening an IEP team meeting.

Amending the IEP

Under the IDEA 2004 the parents and the school district can agree to change the IEP and agree NOT to convene an IEP team meeting to make the changes. If the parents and district both agree, changes to the IEP can be documented in writing and the IEP amended without redrafting the entire IEP. If they request it, the parents must be provided with a copy of the revised IEP that includes the amendments.[126] Note that the IEP cannot be amended without an IEP meeting unless the parents and the school district both agree.

> If the parents and district both agree, changes to the IEP can be documented in writing and the IEP amended without redrafting the entire IEP.

---

[124] 20 U.S.C. 1414(d)(1)(A)(VII)
[125] 20 U.S.C. 1414(d)(4)
[126] 20 U.S.C. 1414(d)(3)(D) and (F)

When both the parents and district agree, amending the IEP without convening an IEP team meeting can be an efficient way to adapt the IEP to meet the student's needs. But changing the IEP without a team meeting may cause confusion regarding what is and is not included in the student's IEP. Parents and school staff, therefore, should make sure that everyone involved understands how the IEP is being amended and that the amendments are clearly documented.

Using the IEP Process

The IEP is both a planning and a communication tool. The IEP process, when done properly, is an excellent way to design programs for students with disabilities. Again, an important first step in the process is ensuring that sufficient assessment data has been collected in all the appropriate areas in which the student may have educational needs, including assistive technology.

In a properly run IEP meeting, the team always focuses the discussion on the unique needs of that particular student. If the needs of other students or the administrative needs of the education staff creep into the discussion, the meeting can get off track and may result in a poor plan. It isn't that the needs of other students or the administration are not important. They are important, but the purpose of the IEP meeting is to discuss the unique needs of the individual student with a disability. If the team focuses on resources needed to serve other students, or administrative/logistical problems involved in providing services, the team will be tempted to limit recommendations for services needed by this particular student.

The IEP is also an excellent communication tool. At the end of the meeting, the parents and others involved in educating the student will have a document that specifically identifies the student's current abilities, educational needs, goals and objectives, and specific services to meet those identified needs, goals and objectives. Everyone involved will know when the services will begin, how often they will be provided, how long they will last, and where they will be provided. Anyone looking at that particular student's IEP will be able to gather that basic information.

A properly written IEP can, therefore, prevent misunderstandings regarding the services a student is to receive. Preventing misunderstandings helps assure that the student actually receives the services the student should receive. Good communication through the IEP process can also prevent misunderstandings that might lead to due process hearings or other dispute resolution procedures. At first glance, the requirements of the IEP process may seem time consuming for school districts, but the time needed to properly write an IEP is time well spent.

Hints for Parents

The parents are equal members of the IEP team and have the right to participate fully in the meeting. Parents have the right to ask questions of other participants in the meeting. If parents choose, they may bring someone, even an attorney, to assist them in the IEP meeting. It is rarely necessary for parents to bring a lawyer to

> The parents are equal members of the IEP team and have the right to participate fully in the meeting. Parents have the right to ask questions of other participants in the meeting.

an IEP meeting, but it might be very helpful for the parents to bring someone to support and assist them in the IEP meeting.

While teachers and other educational staff usually try to focus on the strengths of students, IEP meetings can sometimes center on the problems the student has or may be causing. Thus, a parent, who may have been looking forward to the meeting in the hope that a successful program will be developed, may become disheartened listening to a seemingly endless litany of one problem after another. It isn't hard to imagine that the parent may tend to withdraw from the process or become angry. There are very few things in this world that are more painful than hearing negative comments about one's own child. Although whoever is chairing the IEP meeting should try to avoid this scenario, an advocate or support person may be very useful to help the parent and other members of the team refocus and get the meeting on a more positive track.

Parents may have very valid reasons for getting angry at an IEP meeting. As noted, other members of the team may have made negative comments about the student. Even if such comments are unintentional, they may still be hurtful. Perhaps the IEP hasn't been adequately complied with in the past and the student hasn't received needed services. Or, perhaps designing a program for this particular individual is very difficult due to the nature or severity of the student's disability, so that, despite everyone's best efforts, the process has been frustrating.

Maybe a general education teacher or administrator, unfamiliar with the IDEA, has made an inappropriate comment to the effect: "We don't have to do that for your child." Or, "If we do that for your child, we'll have to cut services

for other kids." While parents have valid reasons to become angry, parents should try not to "lose their cool." Obviously, keeping cool is easier said than done, but sometimes team members can't see through the anger. The views of parents who are perceived as too angry may be discounted. My message to parents is not that they should not get angry, but that they try to keep the anger in check. Keep cool.

If parents have any questions at all, they should raise them at the meeting. For example, if the meeting begins and all the assessment data are not available, the parents should feel free to request that the meeting be rescheduled for a later date when all the data will be available. Without the proper assessment information, the team cannot properly develop the IEP. In most circumstances, whoever chairs the IEP meeting should reschedule it for a time when sufficient data has been collected. But if they do not reschedule the meeting, the parent should bring it to the team's attention.

Parents should prepare for the IEP meeting. A little preparation will go a long way toward increasing the parents' ability to participate in the meeting. Parents should review assessment information and the current IEP to prepare for developing a new IEP. Parents should make a list of all the things they have questions about or that are causing them concern.

It's worth repeating that parents should not go alone to an IEP meeting. While school personnel often try to support parents, encountering a roomful of teachers and other professionals can be intimidating. If possible, parents should take someone with them to help. If parents are assisted by an advocate, they should share their questions with that individual and discuss the upcoming IEP meeting.

The IEP meeting is the appropriate place to discuss any issues related to developing the student's educational program. If the parents have support for their view from an independent educator, therapist, or other professional, it is very helpful to bring that individual to the IEP meeting. That provides an opportunity for the other members of the IEP team to hear that professional's views directly and to ask questions. If it isn't possible to bring the independent professional to the meeting, then bringing their report would be the next best thing.

Finally, at the end of the meeting or meetings, if an IEP has been written, the parents should make sure the IEP includes what was discussed and agreed to. Parents should leave the meeting with a copy of the IEP.

Hints for Educators and Other Members of the IEP Team

First and foremost, remember whose kid it is! The teachers and administrators from the school district have an obligation to ensure the IEP is designed to ensure the student receives a free appropriate public education. School district personnel take that obligation seriously. But the student is not their child. The school district will not be forever responsible for serving the student, but the student's parents will be forever the parents. Much of special education is not an exact science. There are times when the absolute best course of action may be uncertain. In those circumstances, why not agree with the parents' wishes?

Second, listen, listen, and listen. Hear what the parents and what the individuals they have invited to the meeting have to say. Don't cut the discussion short or set an arbitrary time limit to finish the meeting. A special education director

announcing at the start of the IEP meeting that they have only scheduled an hour and a half for the meeting sets the wrong tone. To be sure, there are occasions when there is a need for a time limit for the meeting. Perhaps some team members are only available for a limited amount of time that day. But, they can usually schedule another meeting if the process is not completed in the allotted time. Moreover, the IDEA 2004 has allowed flexibility so that if the parents consent, staff members can be excused from attending all or part of the meeting and can then give input through a written report, if necessary.[127]

Third, be open to answering questions and don't become defensive if your recommendations are questioned. Be open to the parents seeking advice from independent professionals and bringing those individuals to the meeting. The IEP process is meant to be a discussion, with the parents asking questions of the educators, educators asking questions of each other, and even educators asking questions of the parent. That's the process. Part of being a professional is being open to an open discussion.

Finally, as I suggested to parents, avoid getting angry. Don't lose your cool. Certainly, there are times when parents are mistaken or misinformed about what they are asking for and difficult in how they ask for it. But getting angry will only make the situation worse. Be professional, considerate, and courteous. Rude and inconsiderate behavior is the root of many disputes and due process hearings. Just because we're adults doesn't mean our feelings can't get hurt. Hurt feelings can make a mole hill of a disagreement into a mountain of a due process hearing.

---

[127] 20 U.S.C. 1414(d)(1)(C)

Conclusion

Appropriate, like beauty, is in the eye of the beholder. All the participants in the IEP meeting, therefore, should take full advantage of that opportunity to design a program that will meet the unique needs of the student with a disability. The IEP process works when it is done properly. In order for the process to work, the participants need to be prepared for the meeting and contribute to the discussion. Asking questions contributes to the meeting. Each member of the team can contribute to what makes up an appropriate program for the student. Again, parents are experts on their child, and adequate preparation will help parents share their expertise with other members of the IEP team.

The parents are members of the IEP team, but they cannot veto the recommendations of all the other members. The IEP team makes decisions based on a consensus. A consensus means the group has general agreement on the IEP. General agreement doesn't mean unanimous agreement. Some individuals may not fully agree with the IEP at the end of the meeting. If, at the end of the meeting,

the parents disagree with the recommended program, they have the right to appeal that recommendation. For example, if the parents wanted speech therapy to be included as a related service on the IEP, and the team did not include it, then the parents have the right to challenge the IEP through the appeal process.

Parents have the right to request a due process hearing and have an impartial hearing officer resolve the disagreement. There are also other less formal options to resolve disputes available to parents. All of these procedures will be discussed in the next chapter. If the parents disagree with the recommended IEP, but choose not to appeal, the school district can go ahead and implement the IEP.

> Appropriate, like beauty, is in the eye of the beholder. All the participants in the IEP meeting, therefore, should take full advantage of that opportunity to design a program that will meet the unique needs of the student with a disability.

Notes

V Resolving Disputes under the IDEA

Throughout all of the procedures we have discussed to this point, there may be disagreements. The parents may disagree with the educators, the educators may disagree with the parents, and the educators may disagree among themselves. While many educational plans will be developed harmoniously, conflict may arise in the evaluation, re-evaluation, and IEP development process. That conflict should not be unexpected or feared. Serious disagreements may arise even when the IEP process is working perfectly and all participants are doing their best. Disagreement does not mean disaster. Differences don't mean failure. The IDEA expects that team members will not always see eye to eye on the IEP.

The IDEA 2004 offers additional opportunities for parents and school districts to resolve disputes before actually convening a due process hearing. Under the IDEA 2004, any dispute, including issues that happened before a due process complaint has been filed, can be mediated. Mediation agreements have to be in writing and can be enforced in court.

Additionally, before a due process hearing can be convened, a due process complaint notice must be sent to either the school district or the parent, depending on which one is requesting the hearing. The due process complaint notice tells the other side what the issues are and what is needed to resolve the dispute. This might help get the issues resolved before the hearing.

> While many educational plans will be developed harmoniously, conflict may arise in the evaluation, re-evaluation, and IEP development process.

Moreover, a resolution session between the parents and the school district is now required before the hearing occurs. This is true unless the parents and school district agree to waive (or not use) the resolution session or agree to try mediation instead. The mediation, resolution session, and due process hearing procedures will be discussed more fully later in this Chapter, but first let's look at some informal ways to resolve disputes.

The IEP Process

The IEP process itself offers opportunities to resolve conflicts and disagreements. As noted in the previous chapter, the IEP meeting is an excellent place to ask questions, discuss issues, and iron out disagreements. All of the participants in the IEP meeting should raise their concerns and try to get them resolved at the meeting. But sometimes issues cannot be resolved at the meeting.

For example, parents may strongly believe that the assessment data indicates their child needs an adapted wheelchair as an assistive technology device, but school personnel disagree that the wheelchair is needed for the child to benefit from the educational program. The fact the issue is not resolved to everyone's satisfaction at the meeting doesn't mean the process isn't working. It means we may need to try to resolve the dispute through another means.

Sometimes the IEP is agreed upon, but there are disputes regarding how it is being implemented, or even, whether it is being implemented. For example, the IEP may indicate that the student needs to have a tape recorder, but the parents later find out that a tape recorder was never provided. Perhaps the tape recorder is provided, but it isn't provided in all of the student's classes as required by the IEP.

Maybe the tape recorder was provided through the first semester, but it hasn't been provided since the holidays, and the IEP specifically indicated that the duration for this assistive technology service was the entire school year.

These are all clear violations of the IDEA, because, as we know, services are to be provided as specified in the IEP, including the specified frequency and duration of the service. There are a variety of ways, both formal and informal, to resolve these kinds of disputes.

Informal Dispute Resolution Procedures

Informal dispute resolution procedures usually involve writing to, and/or talking with school personnel. Parents might try discussing the issue with teachers, principals, and school administrators. Many school districts have their own written informal appeal procedures.

These procedures usually begin with the parents requesting a conference with the director of special education. If the issue is not resolved in the meeting with the special education director, then the district's policies might allow for a higher level review with the district superintendent. These procedures may vary from school district to school district, so parents should get a copy of the informal procedures used in their particular school district.

Many disagreements may be resolved through these more informal methods. In particular, most Directors of Special Education, if informed that an IEP wasn't being implemented, would make sure that the IEP was being implemented as soon as possible.

Parents, however, are not required to use the school district's informal procedures to resolve disputes. They may proceed directly to the formal process by requesting a due process hearing. Parents may also start to resolve the disagreement informally, but later request a due process hearing if they no longer want to use the informal process. Informal settlement negotiations can still continue after a hearing has been requested. In fact, most cases in which a hearing is requested are settled through negotiation before the hearing begins.

Procedural Safeguards

Under the IDEA school districts must provide extensive protections called procedural safeguards for the educational rights of parents and of students with disabilities. An important part of those protections is the requirement to tell parents what their rights are under the IDEA. Without information about their rights, parents cannot be effective advocates.

To that end, school districts must provide two different types of **notices** to parents. School districts must provide (1) a **prior written notice** to parents when the school district takes or refuses to take certain actions, and (2) a **procedural safeguards notice** at least once a year. The procedural safeguards notice must also be provided when the parents request it, when a complaint is filed, or when the student is being referred for an initial evaluation to determine eligibility for special education services.

> An important part of those protections is the requirement to tell parents what their rights are under the IDEA. Without information about their rights, parents cannot be effective advocates.

On the other hand, parents must provide the school district with a **due process complaint notice** when the parents wish to request a due process hearing. Each of these notices will be discussed in this chapter.

Prior Written Notice

Whenever the school district intends to change the student's educational placement, identification, evaluation, or how the district provides the student a free appropriate public education the school district must notify the student's parents, in writing, about the district's proposed changes. Additionally, if the student's parents ask for a change in the student's identification, evaluation, educational placement, or how the student is provided a free appropriate public education, and the school district refuses to make the change, the school district must also notify the student's parents.[128] This notice to the student's parents is called prior written notice.

The prior notice must be in writing and contain the following information:

1. A description of the action proposed or refused by the school district;

2. An explanation of why the school district proposes or refuses to take the action. The district must also include a description of each evaluation procedure, assessment, record, or report to the school district used as a reason for the proposed action or refused action;

3. A statement that the parents have protections (procedural safeguards) and how to get a copy of the procedural

---

[128] 20 U.S.C. 1415(b)(3)

safeguards (if the prior notice involves an initial referral for evaluation, a copy of the procedural safeguards must be included with the notice);

4. Sources where the parents may be able to get help in understanding the prior notice;

5. A description of the options the IEP team considered and the reason why those options were rejected; and

6. A description of the factors that are relevant to the school district's decision.[129]

The prior written notice gives parents the information they need to understand why the school district is or is not taking a certain action. This information should help the parents understand the reason for the school district's decision and give them information that can be used to ask questions. The better everyone understands the reason for the decision, the more likely it is that the disagreements can be avoided or resolved early on in the process.

Procedural Safeguards Notice

The procedural safeguards notice tells parents about their rights. School districts must give parents the procedural safeguards notice: (1) when the student is referred for an initial evaluation or the parent requests an evaluation; (2) the first time the parent files a complaint about the identification, evaluation, educational placement of the student or the provision of a free appropriate public education to the student; and (3) if the parent requests the notice.

The procedural safeguards notice must include a full explanation of the procedural safeguards. The notice needs to be easily understandable

and, to that end, it must be in the parents' native language (unless it is clearly not feasible to provide it in the parents' native language). The procedural safeguards notice must include information about

1. Independent educational evaluation;

2. Prior written notice;

3. Parental consent;

4. Access to educational records;

5. The opportunity to present and resolve complaints, including

    a. the time period to make a complaint;

    b. the opportunity for the school district to resolve the complaint; and

    c. the availability of mediation;

6. The student's placement while a due process hearing is proceeding;

7. Procedures for students who are subject to placement in an interim alternative educational setting under the IDEA's procedures for disciplining students with disabilities;

8. Requirements for unilateral placement by parents in private schools at public expense;

9. Due process hearings, including the requirements for disclosing evaluation results and recommendations;

The procedural safeguards notice
tells parents about their rights.

---

[129] 20 U.S.C. 1415(c)(1)

10. State-level appeals (if the state has a state-level appeal);

11. Civil actions (law suits), including the time period to file a civil action; and

12. Attorney's fees.[130]

The procedural safeguards notice provides parents with the information they need if they disagree with actions of the school district or decisions of the IEP team. While at first glance, the amount of information school districts are required to provide to parents as part of this notice may seem onerous, this information is essential if parents are to be able to effectively protect their child's right to a free appropriate public education.

Parents have the right to have an impartial due process hearing to resolve any complaints relating to the identification, evaluation, or educational placement of their child, or the provision of a free appropriate public education to the child.[131]

Surrogate Parents

Some children with disabilities do not have parents or their parents cannot be located. Since a child's right to a free appropriate public education under the IDEA is generally protected through parent advocacy, children without parents would be missing an important protection. Congress was conscious of this concern and included in the IDEA's procedural safeguards a process for appointing a *surrogate parent* to act on behalf of students with disabilities under these circumstances.

Consequently, whenever the parents of a child are unknown, can't be located, or the child is a ward of the State, an individual must be assigned to act as a surrogate for the parents in

the education process. To ensure objectivity, the individual appointed to act as the surrogate parent cannot be "an employee of the State Education Agency, the *local education agency*, or any other agency that is involved in the education or care of the child."[132]

Note that the surrogate parent cannot be an employee of "any other agency that is involved in the education or care of the child." Children with disabilities who do not have parents are often in the care of departments of social services and similar agencies. Since those agencies are involved in the care of the child, social workers employed by such agencies are not eligible to act as surrogate parents on behalf of the child.

That does not mean that a social worker assigned to help a child in these circumstances could not attend an IEP meeting or other educational meetings, if appropriate, on behalf of the child. In fact, the social worker would likely be very helpful in the educational planning process. But the social worker cannot be the surrogate parent.

The state must make reasonable efforts to ensure the surrogate is appointed within **30 days** of determining the child needs a surrogate par-

> ...whenever the parents of a child are unknown, can't be located, or the child is a ward of the State, an individual must be assigned to act as a surrogate for the parents in the education process.

---

[130] 20 U.S.C. 1415(d)(2)
[131] 20 U.S.C. 1415(b)(6)(A)
[132] 20 U.S.C. 1415(b)(2)(A)

ent.[133] The surrogate parent has all of the rights that any parent would have to act on behalf of the child with a disability. The surrogate parent has the authority to consent to assessments and placement in special education, review educational records, attend IEP meetings, and pursue dispute resolution procedures, including due process hearings.

Impartial Due Process Hearings

Due Process Complaint Notice

We have just discussed two different types of notice; prior written notice and the procedural safeguards notice. These notices (1) tell parents what the school district is or is not doing and why, and (2) tell parents what their rights are in the process. The prior written notice and procedural safeguards notice are notices that school districts provide to parents. A third type of notice is the due process complaint notice. When either a parent or school district wants to request a due process hearing to resolve a dispute, the due process complaint notice is a notice that must be provided to the other side in the dispute.[134] The due process complaint notice tells the school district or the parent, who the student is, what the issues are, and suggests ways to resolve the dispute.

Note that **school districts** as well as parents can request a due process hearing. For the sake of simplicity, and because most hearings are requested by parents, the discussion in this chapter regarding hearings and other dispute resolution procedures will be discussed primarily from the parents' perspective. Thus, be mindful, that while the discussion below

describes the process when a parent is requesting a hearing, the rights, requirements, and timelines (regarding responses to the notice, amending the notice, mediation, resolution session, and due process hearings and appeals) are generally the same when the school district requests the hearing.

Before parents pursue a due process hearing, the IDEA 2004 requires that the parents send a due process complaint notice to the school district and the State Education Agency. This is a change from the IDEA 97.

Previously, under the IDEA 97, parents were required to send a notice to the school district about problems and proposed resolutions, but the parents could still have a due process hearing even if the notice was not sent. Now, under the IDEA 2004, the parents or their attorney must send the due process complaint notice.[135]

The due process complaint notice gives the school district, or the State Education Agency, a chance to resolve the problem before there is a due process hearing. This notice from the parents that they have a complaint is confidential, must be written, and it must include

1. the student's name, address, and the name of the school the student attends;

2. a description of the nature of the problem including the facts relating to the problem; and

> Before parents pursue a due process hearing, the IDEA 2004 requires that the parents send a due process complaint notice to the school district and the State Education Agency.

---

[133] 20 U.S.C. 1415(b)(2)(A) and (B)
[134] 20 U.S.C. 1415(b)(7)(A) and (B)
[135] 20 U.S.C. 1415(b)(7)(B)

3. a proposed resolution of the problem to the extent the parents know about a possible resolution at the time they file the due process complaint notice.

As noted above, the due process complaint notice is now required to be sent before a due process hearing can be convened. Accordingly, State Education Agencies are required to develop a model form for the due process complaint notice.[136] A sample due process complaint notice is included as Appendix B. While this notice contains all of the IDEA's requirements, the reader should check to determine whether their particular State Education Agency has developed a particular form for the notice.

The content of the due process complaint notice is very important. Parents cannot raise issues at the due process hearing that were not identified in the due process complaint notice unless the school district agrees.[137]

As we will see, the due process complaint notice can be amended to add issues. Parents can also request a separate due process complaint on an issue that is separate from the due process complaint they have already filed.[138] Thus, if an issue comes up that was not included in the due process complaint notice, and the school district does not agree to let the new issue be a part of the current hearing, the parents may request a separate hearing on that issue. In that event, it might be more efficient and economical for the school district to agree to include the new issue in the current hearing.

Response to the Due Process Complaint Notice

There are two ways the school district can respond to the Due Process Complaint Notice.

The school district can (1) respond to the specific issues identified in the Due Process Complaint Notice and/or (2) tell the hearing officer that the school district believes the Due Process Complaint Notice is not sufficient because the notice doesn't have all of the required information. The school district is required to respond to the specific issues identified in the Due Process Complaint Notice, but telling the hearing officer that the notice is insufficient is at the district's discretion.

Response to the Specific Issues Raised in the Due Process Complaint Notice

As noted above, the school district is required to send the parent the school district's response to the specific issues identified in the complaint.[139] This response should address each of the issues raised in the Due Process Complaint Notice. The response must be sent within **10 days** of receiving the Due Process Complaint Notice.[140]

Additionally, if the school district has not already sent the prior written notice information discussed above, the district must include that information in its response. If that is the case, the school district's response must contain all of the information required in a prior written notice regarding the reasons the school district is making a change or refusing to make a change requested by the parents.[141]

---

[136] 20 U.S.C. 1415(b)(8)
[137] 20 U.S.C. 1415(f)(3)(B)
[138] 20 U.S.C. 1415(o)
[139] 20 U.S.C. 1415(c)(2)(B)(ii)
[140] 20 U.S.C. 1415(c)(2)(B)(ii)
[141] 20 U.S.C. 1415(c)(2)(B)(i)(I)

Sufficiency of the Due Process Complaint Notice

If the school district believes the Due Process Complaint Notice doesn't contain all of the information that is legally required or doesn't have enough information, then the school district can inform the hearing officer that the district believes the Due Process Complaint Notice is insufficient. The school district has **15 days** from the time it receives the parent's Due Process Complaint Notice to inform the hearing officer that the district believes the notice is insufficient.[142]

The hearing officer then has **five days** after receiving a notice that the Due Process Complaint Notice is insufficient to decide whether or not it is sufficient. The hearing officer is supposed to decide the sufficiency of the Due Process Complaint Notice "on the face of the notice." This implies that the hearing officer only looks at the notice; the hearing officer does not look at other evidence to decide whether the notice is sufficient.[143]

Amending the Due Process Complaint Notice

If the parents are concerned that their Due Process Complaint Notice might not be sufficient or the parents want to include additional issues or information, they can amend or modify the notice. The Due Process Complaint Notice can be amended if (1) the school district consents in writing and still has a chance to resolve the amended complaint through a resolution meeting, or (2) the hearing officer grants permission to amend the Due Process Complaint Notice.

The hearing officer can grant permission to amend the notice anytime, but not later than **five days** before the hearing.[144] If the Due Process Complaint Notice is amended, then the timeline for the hearing starts over at the time the amended notice is filed.[145]

Mediation

As discussed at the beginning of this chapter, the IDEA 2004 provides a resolution session and mediation as additional opportunities for parents and school districts to resolve disputes. Mediation is a process in which an objective and neutral third party (the mediator) works with both sides of a dispute to help them reach an agreement.

The mediator does not weigh evidence or determine legal issues. Deciding legal issues and weighing evidence is the job of a hearing officer. The mediator's job is to help the two sides to reach an agreement that ends the dispute.

Under the IDEA 2004, State Education Agencies and school districts must have procedures that allow parents and school districts to be able to mediate any issue, including issues that occur before a Due Process Complaint is filed. This means that parents and school districts can try to mediate disputes without requesting a due process hearing.[146]

---

[142] 20 U.S.C. 1415(c)(2)(A) and (C)
[143] 20 U.S.C. 1415(c)(2)(D)
[144] 20 U.S.C. 1415(c)(2)(E)
[145] 20 U.S.C. 1415(c)(2)(E)(ii)
[146] 20 U.S.C. 1415(e)(1)

Mediation is a process in which an objective and neutral third party (the mediator) works with both sides of a dispute to help them reach an agreement.

Participation in mediation is voluntary by both sides and completely optional. Moreover, the procedures adopted by school districts and the State Education Agency must ensure that mediation is not used to deny or delay a parent's right to a due process hearing.[147] Thus, by agreeing to mediation, neither the parents nor the school district give up the right to pursue an impartial due process hearing. Mediation could be attempted before a hearing is requested or after a hearing has been requested and a last effort is being made to resolve the dispute. In either case, if the mediation is unsuccessful, either side can request a hearing, or the case can continue toward a hearing.

The discussions that occur during mediation, however, are confidential and cannot be used later as evidence in a due process hearing or lawsuit.[148] The confidentiality of the mediation discussions is important. For the mediator to be effective, both sides must be able to speak freely in the mediation discussion.

Obviously, the success of the mediation process is closely linked to the skills and training of the mediator. To that end, the IDEA requires that the mediation be conducted by a qualified and impartial mediator who is trained in effective mediation techniques.[149] Accordingly, the State Education Agency must maintain a list of mediators who are qualified as mediators and know about special education law.[150]

Finally, the State Education Agency is responsible for the costs of the mediation process.[151]Presumably, the State's obligation is to cover the costs of the mediator, not the costs to the school district or the parents for their time or the costs of their lawyers, if they choose to be represented by lawyers.

Resolution through Mediation Is Legally Binding

In the past some parents and school districts have been reluctant to mediate disputes out of concern that, even if an agreement is reached, the other side will not live up to their end of the bargain. To help relieve this concern, the IDEA 2004 requires that if an agreement is reached, it is legally binding.[152]

Accordingly, the IDEA requires that if the dispute is resolved through mediation, the two sides make a legally binding agreement. The legally binding agreement must (1) state that the discussions in the mediation are confidential and can't be used as evidence in a hearing or lawsuit; (2) be signed by both the parents and a representative of the school district who has the authority to bind the school district to the agreement; and (3) be enforceable in State court or a United States district court.[153]

> In the past some parents and school districts have been reluctant to mediate disputes out of concern that, even if an agreement is reached, the other side will not live up to their end of the bargain. To help relieve this concern, the IDEA 2004 requires that if an agreement is reached, it is legally binding.

[147] 20 U.S.C. 1415(e)(2)(A)(ii)
[148] 20 U.S.C. 1415(e)(2)(G)
[149] 20 U.S.C. 1415(e)(2)(A)(iii)
[150] 20 U.S.C. 1415(e)(2)(C)
[151] 20 U.S.C. 1415(e)(2)(D)
[152] 20 U.S.C. 1415(e)(2)(F)
[153] 20 U.S.C. 1415(e)(2)(F)

*Mediation Means Finding a
Middle Course*

The mediation process is less formal and less legalistic than the impartial hearing process. Parents can bring a lawyer, but the focus of the discussion is on resolving the dispute, not on the legal arguments of the two sides. There is a meeting, rather than a hearing. No witnesses are called and no evidence is introduced. The mediator helps both sides to get to the bottom of the problem.

Mediation is an excellent way to resolve many disagreements. Remember, however, that mediation is entirely optional and voluntary. In fact, for mediation to work, it can't be forced on one side or the other. Both sides must be open to trying to resolve the dispute. Mediation means finding a middle course. If both sides are willing, a skilled mediator can help them find that middle course.

Resolution Session

The IDEA 2004 has added a resolution session as yet another way to resolve disputes before a due process hearing is convened. Once a Due Process Hearing Complaint has been filed, but

> Once a Due Process Hearing Complaint has been filed, but before the hearing occurs, the school district is required to convene a meeting with the parents and the relevant member or members of the IEP team to try to resolve the dispute.

before the hearing occurs, the school district is required to convene a meeting with the parents and the relevant member or members of the IEP team to try to resolve the dispute.

The relevant members of the IEP team are the members of the IEP team who have specific knowledge of the facts identified in the Due Process Hearing Complaint. The meeting must also include a representative of the school district who has the authority to make decisions on behalf of the school district.

The meeting may NOT include an attorney representing the school district unless the parents bring an attorney to the meeting. If the parents, however, do bring an attorney to the meeting and the complaint is resolved, the parents are not entitled to be reimbursed for the attorney's time for attending the resolution session.[154] The purpose of the meeting is for the parents to be able to discuss their complaint and to give the school district a chance to resolve it.[155]

This resolution session is required unless the parents and the school district agree in writing to waive it or the two sides agree to use mediation instead. The Resolution Session must be convened within **15 days** of the school district receiving the parent's Due Process Hearing Complaint.[156]

If the school district has not resolved the complaint to the parents' satisfaction within **30 days of** receiving the complaint, then the due process hearing can occur. Moreover, if the complaint is not resolved within the 30 days, the 45-day timeline for the hearing will commence at the end of the 30 days.[157] If the complaint is resolved, the two sides will make a legally binding written agreement resolving the complaint.

[154] 20 U.S.C. 1415(i)(3)(D)(iii)
[155] 20 U.S.C. 1415(f)(1)(B)
[156] 20 U.S.C. 1415(f)(1)(B)(i)(I)
[157] 20 U.S.C. 1415(f)(1)(B)(ii), 34 CFR 300.515

Resolution Session Settlement Agreement

If the parents and the school district resolve the complaint through the Resolution Session, they will develop a written agreement. The written agreement must be signed by both the parent and a representative of the school district who has the authority to bind or commit the school district. The written agreement is enforceable in either State court, or a United States district court.

Each side, however, still has **three business days** after the agreement is signed to void, or get out of, the agreement. **Note the days referred to here are business days, not calendar days.**[158]

Impartial Due Process Hearing

Hearing Issues

The IDEA 2004 has made some significant changes to the due process hearing procedures. As noted earlier, issues that were not identified in the Due Process Complaint Notice cannot be raised at the hearing. Also, the hearing officer's decision must "be made on substantive grounds based on a determination of whether the child received a free appropriate public education."[159]

Generally, this means the hearing officer must make a decision on substantive (actual, fundamental or essential) grounds rather than procedural (directive or functional) grounds. There must be a link between the violation of the IDEA and the student not receiving a free appropriate public education.

Congress was concerned that there had been cases "in which a hearing officer has found that a school denied FAPE to a child with a disability based upon a mere procedural technicality, rather than an actual showing that the child's education was harmed by the procedural flaw. . ."[160]

Congress, however, understood that there are procedural violations that can deny a student a free appropriate public education. "For example, a school's failure to give a parent access to initial evaluation information to make an informed and timely decision about their child's education can amount to a FAPE violation."[161] Therefore, in cases involving a complaint about a procedural violation of the IDEA, the hearing officer may determine the student did not receive a free appropriate public education, but "only if the procedural inadequacies

1. impeded the child's right to a free appropriate public education;

2. significantly impeded the parent's opportunity to participate in the decision-making process regarding the provision of a free appropriate public education to the parent's child; or

3. caused a deprivation of educational benefits."[162]

Timeline for Requesting a Hearing

The IDEA 2004 has a **two-year timeline** for requesting a hearing. Generally, the parent or school district must request a hearing within two years of the date the parent or district "knew or should have known" about the vio-

[158] 20 U.S.C. 1415(f)(1)(B)(iii) and (iv)
[159] 20 U.S.C. 1415(f)(3)(E)
[160] CRS Report for Congress, Individuals with Disabilities Education Act (IDEA): Analysis of Changes Made by P.L. 108-446, Jan. 5, 2005 p. 27, quoting S.Rept. 185, 108th Cong., 1st Sess., 40 (2003)
[161] CRS Report for Congress, Individuals with Disabilities Education Act (IDEA): Analysis of Changes Made by P.L. 108-446, Jan. 5, 2005 p. 27, quoting S.Rept. 185, 108th Cong., 1st Sess., 41 (2003)
[162] 20 U.S.C. 1415(f)(3)(E)(i) and (ii)

Generally, the parent or school district must request a hearing within two years of the date the parent or district "knew or should have known" about the violation that is the basis of the hearing request.

lation that is the basis of the hearing request. This two-year timeline will be applied unless the State has its own explicit timeline for requesting hearings.[163]

The two-year timeline will not apply to a parent, however, if the parent was prevented from requesting a hearing because (1) the school district specifically misrepresented that it had resolved the problem, or (2) the school district withheld information from the parent that the district was required to give to the parent.[164]

Rights in the Hearing Process

Both sides to a hearing, parent and school district, have the following rights in the hearing:

- the right to be accompanied and advised by counsel (lawyer) and by individuals with special knowledge or training with respect to the problems of children with disabilities

- the right to present evidence and confront, cross-examine, and compel the attendance of witnesses

- the right to a written, or, at the option of the parents, electronic verbatim (exact) record of the hearing

- the right to written, or at the option of the parents, electronic findings of fact and decisions[165]

Additionally, not less than **five days** before the hearing, each side must disclose to the other all evaluations that have been completed by that date. Moreover, each side must disclose to the other side recommendations they plan on using at the hearing that are based on those evaluations. If the evaluations and recommendations are not disclosed **five days** before the hearing, the hearing officer may prevent the evaluation or recommendation from being used at the hearing. This is true unless the other side agrees to let the undisclosed evaluation or recommendation be used at the hearing.[166]

Burden of Proof

Burden of proof is a legal term that means which side needs to present more evidence than the other, to win. The IDEA does not mention burden of proof, but the Supreme Court determined in *Schaeffer v. Weast* that the burden of proof in a hearing challenging an IEP is on the side that is challenging the IEP.[167] It is likely that in most special education hearings parents will be challenging the IEP. So, in most hearings parents will have the "burden" to show that the IEP is inappropriate.

In the *Schaeffer v. Weast* decision, the Supreme Court did not decide whether states, through legislation, can place the burden of proof on the school district. Some states may have laws that place the burden of showing that an IEP is appropriate on the school district. So, par-

---

[163] 20 U.S.C. 1415(f)(3)(C)
[164] 20 U.S.C. 1415(f)(3)(D)
[165] 20 U.S.C. 1415(h)
[166] 20 U.S.C. 1415(f)(2)
[167] *Schaeffer v. Weast*, 126 S. Ct. 528 (2005)

ents and attorneys should check their own state law regarding burden of proof. Finally, while to parents it may seem unfair that the burden of proof to show the effectiveness of an IEP is not on the school district, most hearings are not decided on subtle differences in evidence. It's likely that in most cases, which side has the burden of proof is not a critical factor in the hearing officer's decision.

Qualifications of the Hearing Officer

The hearing officer must be impartial. That means the hearing officer cannot have a personal or professional interest that conflicts with the person's objectivity at the hearing.[168] Objectivity means the hearing officer doesn't have any personal or professional bias or prejudice that would affect their judgment regarding the issues in the hearing or the outcome of the hearing. Moreover, the hearing officer cannot be an employee of the State Education Agency or the school district that is involved in the education or care of the student.

Finally, the hearing officer must have the knowledge and ability to understand the provisions of the IDEA and its regulations as well as legal interpretations by the courts in order to conduct hearings according to standard legal practice. The hearing officer must also be able to make and write decisions according to standard legal practice.[169]

Timeline for Hearing Officer Decision

Generally, the hearing officer must make a final decision within **45 calendar days**. As noted in the section on the Resolution Session, this 45-day hearing timeline begins the day after the 30-day time line to resolve the disagreement through the resolution session ends. This is true unless one of the following situations occurs.[170]

- The parents and the school district agree in writing to waive (not have) the resolution meeting. In that case, the 45-day timeline will begin the day after the parents and school district make that agreement.

- The parents and the school district have started mediation or the resolution process, but before the 30-day resolution timeline ends, they both agree in writing that "no agreement is possible". In that case the 45-day timeline for the hearing decision will begin the day after the parents and school district make that agreement that they cannot agree.

- The parents and the school district begin mediation and agree in writing to extend the mediation beyond the 30-day resolution timeline, then either the parents or the school district withdraws (pulls out) from the mediation process. In that case the 45-day hearing timeline will begin the day after either the parent or school district withdraws from the mediation.[171]

Finally, the hearing officer may extend the hearing decision timeline if either the parents or school district request a specific extension of time.[172]

---

[168] 20 U.S.C. 1415(f)(3)(A)(i)(II)
[169] 20 U.S.C. 1415(f)(3)(A)(ii)(iii)(iv)
[170] 34 CFR 300.515(a)
[171] 34 CFR 300.510(c)
[172] 34 CFR 300.515(c)

Appeal Process

Administrative Appeal

Either side can appeal the hearing officer's decision. If the hearing was conducted by the school district at the local level, then the decision can be appealed to the State Education Agency. The State Education Agency must conduct an impartial review of the local level hearing officer's findings and decision and then make an independent decision. In these circumstances, there will be a decision by an impartial hearing officer at the local-level that is reviewed by another official at the state level.[173]

This is generally referred to as a two-tiered or two-level hearing process. The local hearing conducted by the school district is the first tier or level, and the appeal that is reviewed by a state-level official is the second.

In some states the State Education Agency conducts the impartial hearing, not the local school district. In those circumstances, since the State Education Agency conducts the first hearing, a process for reviewing the decision at the state level isn't required. These states have a one-tiered hearing process.

Either side has the right to file a civil action (lawsuit) in state or federal district court to get a court review of the final decision. If the state has a one-tiered process, then the final decision is the decision from that hearing. If the state has a two-tiered process, the final decision will be the second decision made at the state level.[174] Thus, it is important to know if your state has a one-tiered or two-tiered process. Information about the hearing and appeal process must be provided to parents as part of the procedural safeguards notice discussed earlier in this chapter.

Civil Action

As noted, either side can file an action in state or federal district court. The side filing the lawsuit has **90 days from the date of the hearing officer's decision** to file the lawsuit.[175] This **90-day timeline** will apply unless the **state has its own specific timeline** for filing a civil action. If that is the case, the state's specific timeline will apply. In the civil action the court shall receive the records of the administrative hearings, hear additional evidence at the request of either side, and base its decision on a preponderance (majority, outweighing) of the evidence. Finally, the court will grant the relief (remedy, award) the court decides is appropriate.[176] After the state or federal district court makes its decision, either side can appeal further through that particular appeal process.

Attorney's Fees

Parents who win their hearing, or win in the appeal process, may be awarded their attorney's fees.[177] Parents who win their hearing, however, are not entitled to recover the fees they may have paid to their expert witnesses.[178] Moreover, the parents' attorney's fees can be reduced by the court for several reasons. If the attorney for the parents did not provide the written confidential notice discussed previously, the court may reduce the award of attorney's fees.

The court may also reduce the parents' award of attorney's fees if the court determines that

[173] 20 U.S.C. 1415(g)

[174] 20 U.S.C. 1415(i)(1) and (2)

[175] 20 U.S.C. 1415(i)(2)(A)(B)

[176] 20 U.S.C. 1415(i)(C)

[177] 20 U.S.C. 1415(i)(3)(B)

[178] *Arlington Central School District v. Murphy*, 126 S. Ct. 2465 (2006): Note, in Nov. 2007 legislation was introduced in Congress to include expert witness fees as attorney's fees.

the parent or the parent's attorney unreasonably protracted (dragged out) resolving the dispute, if the fees unreasonably exceeded the prevailing rate in the community for similar legal work, or if the time spent and legal services furnished were excessive.[179] But the provisions reducing the parents' attorney's fees do not apply if the court determines that the school district or State Education Agency unreasonably protracted settling the case.

Additionally, attorney's fees may be denied to the parents in some circumstances when the school district has made an offer to settle the case. Attorney's fees may not be awarded to the parents if the parents have rejected an offer of settlement from the school district that was made **10 days** before the hearing started, and the court determines that the results the parents obtained through the hearing or litigation is not better than the district's settlement offer.[180] But if the court decides the parent was substantially justified in rejecting the school district's settlement offer, the court can still award the parents' attorney's fees.[181]

Generally, parents cannot be reimbursed for their attorney's time spent in IEP meetings. This is true unless the IEP meeting was convened as a result of an administrative proceeding (hearing) or judicial (court) action. States can choose whether or not to provide attorney's fees for mediation sessions called as a result of a hearing or litigation.[182] And, as noted earlier, attorney's fees generally cannot be awarded for an attorney's time in the Resolution Session required before a hearing commences.[183]

The IDEA 2004 includes new provisions allowing the school district or State Education Agency to be awarded attorney's fees in certain circumstances. These circumstances generally involve the parent or the parents' attorney (1) filing frivolous (flimsy, insignificant) actions or continuing to litigate after the litigation clearly became frivolous, unreasonable, or unfounded, or (2) filing or pursuing actions for improper purposes such as to harass, to cause unnecessary delay, or to needlessly increase the cost of the litigation.[184]

The Stay-put Rule

Throughout the hearing and the appeal process, the student will "stay-put" in the educational program he or she was in before the request for a hearing was filed.[185] If the student is applying for initial admission to public school, then, with the parents' consent, the school district will admit the student to public school. "Stay-Put" means the student stays in the placement that was defined by the IEP before the dispute began.

For example, a student's IEP currently includes an augmentative communication device as a supplementary aid or service. The IEP team meets, and despite the parents' objection, the team recommends that this device is no longer

> Throughout the hearing and the appeal process, the student will "stay-put" in the educational program he or she was in before the request for a hearing was filed.

[179] 20 U.S.C. 1415(i)(3)(F)
[180] 20 U.S.C. 1415(i)(3)(D)
[181] 20 U.S.C. 1415(i)(3)(E)
[182] 20 U.S.C. 1415(i)(3)(D)(ii)
[183] 20 U.S.C. 1415(i)(3)(D)(iii)
[184] 20 U.S.C. 1415(i)(3)(B)(i)(II)(III)
[185] 20 U.S.C. 1415(j)

needed and deletes it as a service written on the IEP. If the parents request an impartial due process hearing, the IEP that includes the augmentative communication device would remain in effect during the hearing. The student would continue to have access to the augmentative communication device because it was included in the current IEP. The student will stay-put in the current program, unless the school district and the student's parents agree to place the student in another setting during the appeal.

On the other hand, if the student's current IEP did not include the augmentative communication device, and the parents requested a hearing in order to obtain the device, the student's placement during the hearing would be in a program without the augmentative communication device. The student would stay-put in the current IEP program that does not include the augmentative communication device, unless the parents and the school district are able to agree to some other arrangement.

Under the stay-put rule, the student's parents and the school district can still agree to place the student in a setting other than the current program during the appeal process. If they agree to a placement, other than the current placement, the student will stay there during the appeal.

Whether it is the current placement, another placement the parents and district agree upon, or a placement based on a determination by an administrative law judge, the stay-put placement will remain, at least until a district court reaches a decision. If the district court's decision were to be appealed to a higher court, the student would stay in the program outlined in the district court's decision.

There is an exception to the stay-put rule for appeals of changes in placement when students are being disciplined. Please see the chapter on discipline for a discussion of that appeal process and where students are placed during those appeals.

State Education Agency Complaint Process

Still, another way to resolve disputes under the IDEA is by filing a complaint with the State Education Agency. The IDEA regulations require that the State Education Agency has a process to resolve complaints regarding implementing the IDEA.[186] Under this process individuals or organizations may file a complaint for violations of the IDEA with their State Education Agency. Upon receiving a complaint asserting a violation of the IDEA, the State Education Agency may carry out an independent investigation and, if necessary, conduct the investigation at the school or program where the violation may have occurred.

A complaint under the State Education Agency Complaint Process is not the same as the Due Process Complaint Notice that parents are required to file to request a due process hearing. The complaint procedure being discussed in this section involves an investigation by the State Education Agency rather than a hearing with an independent hearing officer. In the course of an investigation the State Education Agency may review documents and interview individuals, but there is not a formal hearing.

If the State Education Agency determines the IDEA was violated and a child was denied appropriate services, it can require the school district to remedy or correct the violation. In order to correct the violation, the State Educa-

---

[186] 34 CFR 300.151

tion Agency can require the school district to provide compensatory services, monetary reimbursement, and/or provide appropriate services in the future.[187]

Compensatory services are services that are provided to make up for or compensate the child for services that legally should have been provided but were not. For example, consider a situation in which a student's IEP clearly stated that the student was to receive physical therapy three times a week, but the physical therapy was never actually provided. To resolve a complaint about the district's failure to provide the required physical therapy, the State Education Agency could require the school district to provide additional therapy services beyond those required by the IEP. These additional services would be "compensatory" because they are intended to compensate or make up for the services that were not provided.

Or, perhaps the child's parents had privately purchased physical therapy services for their child during the time the school district was not providing the physical therapy services as required by the IEP. In that circumstance the State Education Agency might require the school district to reimburse the parents the money they paid for the private physical therapy. Thus, the parents are provided with monetary reimbursement for the costs of the therapy the parents purchased.

Finally, consider a scenario in which a student's IEP included access to a piece of assistive technology such as a tape recorder to record lectures, but the tape recorder has not been provided. The State Education Agency might order the school district to provide the tape recorder in the future.

The State Education Agency Complaint Process is best used for cases in which the school district has very clearly not complied with the IDEA. For example:

> (1) Services have not been provided as required by an IEP.
>
> (2) The parent has requested that their child be assessed to determine eligibility for special education, and school personnel have not followed through on the assessments.
>
> (3) The school district hasn't responded to a request for an independent evaluation regarding assistive technology issues and hasn't scheduled a hearing to resolve the dispute.
>
> (4) The school district hasn't notified parents of due process procedures.
>
> (5) School personnel have assessed a student without getting the parent's consent.

If the issue involves very clear violations of the IDEA, then the Complaint Process can be useful in getting the school district to comply with the law. On the other hand, if the issue concerns a disagreement over whether a student needs a particular service and the school district refuses to include that service on the IEP, it is difficult for the State Education Agency to resolve that dispute. Determining a student's educational needs requires evidence and the testimony of witnesses. That determination is more appropriate for an impartial hearing officer, who will be able to hear that kind of testimony. The State Education Agency's investigation is mainly limited to reviewing documents and interviewing individuals such as the parents and school staff to determine the facts.

[187] 34 CFR 300.151(b)

Filing a Complaint with the State Education Agency

A complaint may be filed by an individual or an organization. The complaint must be written and signed and contain the following information:

A statement that the public agency has violated the IDEA. Public agencies include school districts, charter schools, the State Education Agency, and other agencies responsible fro providing education to children with disabilities;

The facts that support the above statement that the public agency violated the IDEA;

The signature and contact information of the person making the complaint; If the complaint is regarding a specific child then the complaint must include:

The child's name and address;

The name of the school the child attends;

If the child is homeless the available contact information for the child and the name of the school the child attends;

A description of the problem including facts describing the problem; and

A proposed resolution of the problem to the extent the person filing the complaint knows of a possible resolution of the problem.[188]

Complaints must assert or allege a violation of the IDEA that has occurred within a year of when the complaint is received by the State Education Agency and a copy of the complaint must be sent to the school district or other public agency serving the child at the time the complaint is filed with

[188] 34 CFR 300.153
[189] 34 CFR 300.151(a)(1)(ii)

the State Education Agency. Generally. the IDEA requires that complaints to the State Education Agency be investigated and resolved within 60 days. But in exceptional circumstances that time limit can be extended. Finally, the IDEA provides that the State Education Agency may allow complaints to be filed first with the local school district and the school district's decision reviewed by the State Education Agency.[189] So, parents and other professionals should check with their State Education Agency to determine how the complaint process works in their state.

Thoughts and Hints about Dispute Resolution

As we discussed at the beginning of this chapter, disagreements, disputes and conflict in the special education process should not be unexpected or feared. In fact, if there are never any disagreements, the IEP process and other planning procedures probably aren't being used effectively. We should expect disagreement. Well meaning individuals can have honest differences of opinion about services for students with disabilities. It's through discussing those differences of opinion that we will arrive at an appropriate program for the student. We want an IEP process in which each team member feels free to state their opinions and ask questions of other team members.

Remember, appropriate, like beauty, is in the eye of the beholder. Most often, disagreements can be worked out in the IEP meeting itself, or through informal discussions and dispute resolution procedures.

But there are times when the disagreements do not get resolved, and when more formal procedures may be necessary. In those circumstances, the IDEA 2004 offers additional options such as mediation and the prehearing resolution session to resolve the disagreement. Mediation can be tried even without filing a due process complaint notice and moving towards a hearing. These additional options are good, because everyone involved should want, if at all possible, to resolve the dispute short of a due process hearing and litigation.

Hearings are contentious and adversarial. Hearings are like a trial. Attorneys will put on evidence, call witnesses, and make legal arguments. Hearings are time consuming and costly. Both sides pay for their attorneys. The school district also pays for its staff time and often pays for the cost of the hearing officer. Each side of the dispute should think carefully before going too far down the road to a due process hearing.

Try to look at the dispute both objectively and from the other side's point of view. Play the devil's advocate. Assess the strengths and weaknesses of your position. Parents might try talking to an objective third party, whether it's an attorney or non-attorney advocate. For example, as you can tell from the section of this chapter on the due process complaint notice, that notice and its content are very important. The notice is required, and issues may not be included in the hearing if they are not described in the notice.

So, it is important that the notice is complete and accurately describes the issues. An objective third party can help brainstorm the situa-

tion and clarify the facts and issues. Additionally, the objective advocate can review the draft due process complaint notice to be sure it is understandable and complete.

The due process complaint notice must contain a proposed resolution to the problem. So, it is important to assess what you want to happen to resolve the problem or problems. Even if you are not thinking about requesting a hearing, it is important to ask yourself what needs to happen to resolve the dispute. Don't make decisions when you are angry. While most of the time most educators try to do their best and try to work effectively and courteously with families, there are times when they might not. There are times when parents have every right to be angry. But do not make major decisions when you're angry. Don't let anger cloud your judgment.

Finally, having said that due process hearings are contentious, costly, and adversarial, let me point out that they are also sometimes very necessary. Moreover, because they are contentious, costly, and adversarial, most cases in which a hearing is requested are settled before the hearing occurs. But there are times when the issues are significant and the issues do not get resolved. In those circumstances, a due process hearing is an appropriate way to ensure that a student with a disability receives a free appropriate public education.

Notes

Dispute Resolution Timeline

Due Process Complaint Notice (Complaint) sent by parent to school district.

✗ Note the conflict resolution timelines are triggered by parents sending a due process complaint notice (Complaint).[190] The days referred to in this timeline are calendar days, not school days. The days are counted from the date the school district receives the Complaint.

10 days to respond to Complaint:

The school district has 10 calendar days from receiving the Complaint to send a response that specifically addresses the issues raised in the Complaint.

S	M	T	W	T	F	S
	1 ✗	2	3	4	5	6
7	8	9	10	11	12	13
14	15	16 ☆	17	18	19	20
21	22	23	24	25	26	27
28	29	30	31 ★			

15 days to claim Complaint is insufficient:

The school district has 15 calendar days from receiving the Complaint to notify the hearing officer the school district believes the Complaint is insufficient (does not contain the information required by the IDEA at 20 U.S.C. 1415(b)(7)(A)).

The impartial hearing officer (IHO) has 5 calendar days from the date the IHO received the school district's claim that the Complaint is insufficient to decide if the Complaint is sufficient.

15 days Resolution Session:

 Within 15 days of receiving the Complaint the school district must convene a Resolution Session. The resolution session is a meeting of the parents and the relevant members of the IEP team to try to resolve the Complaint. The Resolution Session must be convened unless the parents and school district agree to waive the meeting or try Mediation instead.

30 days due process hearing timelines commence.

 If the Complaint is not resolved within 30 calendar days of receipt of the Complaint, a due process hearing may occur and the 45-day due process hearing timelines begins.

---

[190] For simplicity this timeline uses an example with parents sending a Due Process Complaint Notice to the school district, but note that school districts may also commence the hearing process by sending a Due Process Complaint Notice to the parents.

VI Discipline and Disability

Like all students, students with disabilities sometimes misbehave. Misbehaving students with disabilities, like all students, may be disciplined. The type of discipline, short or long-term suspension or expulsion, depends on the seriousness of the student's misbehavior. Obviously, disciplining any student for serious misbehavior is an emotional process for parents, teachers, and students. In addition, disciplining students with disabilities is justifiably complicated for two reasons.

First, there are times when a student's conduct may look like misbehavior, but that conduct is actually rooted in the child's disability and entwined with his educational program. The student's behavior is related to his disability. The IDEA recog-

nizes that students with disabilities should not be punished for conduct that is related to their disability. The IDEA does not say that students with disabilities can't be suspended or expelled. They may be suspended or expelled. But students with disabilities may not be expelled for behavior that is related to their disability.[191]

Second, the IDEA requires that all students with disabilities, including those who are sus-

> First, there are times when a student's conduct may look like misbehavior, but that conduct is actually rooted in the child's disability and entwined with his educational program. The student's behavior is related to his disability.

---

[191] *OSEP Memorandum 95-16*, 22 IDELR 531 (OSEP 1995), S-1 v. Turlington, 635 F.2d 342 (5th Cir. 1981)

pended or expelled, must be provided a free appropriate public education.[192]

During long-term suspensions (more than 10 consecutive school days) or expulsions, students with disabilities must continue to receive educational services. This is true because the IDEA requires that all students with disabilities are entitled to a free appropriate public education, including those who have been suspended or expelled.

In the IDEA 97, Congress established specific procedures for disciplining students with disabilities. These procedures tried to balance discipline and the need for safety with the requirements that students with disabilities not be punished for disability-related "misbehavior," and that they continue to receive services during long-term suspensions or expulsions. Thus, the IDEA 97 required that if a student with a disability was removed from his current placement for more than 10 school days that the IEP team must determine if the conduct causing the removal was a **manifestation of the student's disability**.

In the IDEA 2004, Congress revised the disciplinary provisions for students with disabilities. The primary protections for students with disabilities have been maintained. The IDEA

> The IDEA 2004 still requires that if a student is removed for more than 10 days, there be a manifestation determination. But the entire IEP team is no longer required to participate in making the manifestation determination.

2004 still requires that if a student is removed for more than 10 school days, there be a *manifestation determination*. But the entire IEP team is no longer required to participate in making the manifestation determination. Under the IDEA 2004, the school district, the parent, and **relevant members of the IEP team** meet to make the manifestation determination. Additionally, the criteria for determining whether the conduct constitutes a manifestation have been changed. This chapter will review the IDEA's disciplinary procedures and point out where the IDEA 2004 has made changes from the IDEA 97.

Discipline Overview

This section will provide an overview of the disciplinary process for students with disabilities under the IDEA 2004. Some of the terms and procedures covered in this section may be unfamiliar or seem confusing at first glance. Don't worry. After I cover the big picture through the overview, I will go back and cover concepts like manifestation determination, **special circumstances, interim alternative educational setting, and authority of school personnel** in more detail.

Schools and school districts have written rules regarding student behavior. These rules tell students what is considered misconduct. These rules are generally referred to as a code of student conduct. The disciplinary provisions of the IDEA 2004 spell out the authority of school personnel to **remove** a student from the student's **current placement** when he violates a code of student conduct. For simplicity, we will refer to a violation of a code of student conduct as "misconduct." Keep in mind that the IDEA's disciplinary provisions allow school officials to remove a student with

[192] 20 U.S.C. 1412(a)(1)(A) and see *Honig v. Doe*, 484 U.S. 305 (1988)

a disability for a violation of a code of student conduct, and I am using the term "misconduct" to refer to that violation.

School personnel have the authority to remove a student for misconduct from the student's current placement to an interim alternative setting, **another setting, or through suspension**. The initial removal cannot be **more than 10 school days**. During the initial 10 school day removal, the school district is not required to provide services to the student.

True, all students with disabilities must be provided a free appropriate public education, including those who are suspended or expelled, but the IDEA is making an exception for students who are removed for 10 school days or less. If the school district intends to remove the student for more than 10 school days, the district will have to provide educational services for the student in an interim alternative educational setting. This placement is sometimes referred to as the IAES.

There are **special circumstances** that allow the school district to remove a student with a disability for more than the initial 10 school days. Generally, special circumstances, involve possession of a weapon, the use or possession of illegal drugs, or situations in which the student has seriously injured another person. Under those circumstances the student can be removed for no more than 45 school days. But if the student is removed for more than 10 school days, that extended removal is considered a **change in placement**. A change of placement also occurs if the student "has been subjected to a series of removals that constitute a pattern."[193] A series of removals are a pattern if: (1) they total more than 10 school days in a school year (2) the

student's behavior is substantially similar to his behavior in previous incidents when he was removed, and (3) considering other factors like the length of each removal, the total amount of time the student has been removed, and the proximity of the removals to one another, there appears to be a pattern of removing the student.[194]

If there is a change in placement, the school district must (1) do a manifestation determination, (2) provide an educational program, and, (3) as appropriate, provide a *functional behavioral assessment* and behavior intervention services and modifications. These three elements are described below.

Manifestation Determination

The manifestation determination is made by the school district, the parents, and relevant members of the IEP team. The parents and the school district determine which members of the IEP team are relevant and to be included in the manifestation determination meeting. Unless special circumstances exist, if the student's behavior is determined to be a manifestation of the student's disability, the student is returned to his current placement. The parents and the school district, however, can agree to a different placement for the student.

On the other hand, if the student's behavior is determined NOT to be a manifestation of the student's disability, the student may be disciplined in the same manner the school district would discipline a student without a disability for the same behavior. The school district, however, cannot cease providing educational services to the student with a disability. Thus,

---

[193] 34 CFR 300.536
[194] 34 CFR 300.536(a)(2)

> ...if the student is removed for more than 10 school days, the student must continue to receive educational services during the removal.

a student with a disability can be expelled for misbehavior if the behavior is not a manifestation of the student's disability. But while the student serves his time in expulsion, he is placed in an interim alternative educational setting to continue receiving a free appropriate public education.

Provision of Educational Services

Remember, if the student is removed for more than 10 school days, the student must continue to receive educational services during the removal.[195] This is because all students with a disability must receive a free appropriate public education, including students who are suspended or expelled.[196] When a student is removed for more than 10 school days, the IEP team must determine an interim alternative educational setting for the student. The student will receive his educational services in that setting during the extended removal.

> A functional behavioral assessment gathers information about the student's behavior to try to determine what function or purpose the behavior serves for the student.

[195] 20 U.S.C. 1415(k)(1)(C)(D)(E)
[196] 20 U.S.C. 1412(a)(1)(A)
[197] 20 U.S.C. 1415(k)(1)(D)

Functional Behavioral Assessment

While in this interim alternative educational setting, the student should receive, if appropriate, a functional behavioral assessment. The functional behavioral assessment is sometimes referred to as the FBA. A functional behavioral assessment gathers information about the student's behavior to try to determine what function or purpose the behavior serves for the student. The functional behavioral assessment is then used to develop a *behavioral intervention plan*, sometimes referred to as a BIP.

The behavioral intervention plan will describe interventions and modifications designed to teach new, more appropriate behaviors. These behavioral intervention and modification services are designed to address the behavior so that it doesn't happen again.[197]

That's an overview of the process. Now let's take a look at more specific information.

Authority of School Personnel

Schools have rules called **codes of student conduct**. If the punishment for violating the code of student conduct is suspension, then school personnel may suspend a student who violates the code of student conduct for up to 10 school days. If the punishment for misconduct is expulsion, the school district may expel a student with a disability, but not for behavior related to the disability and not without school services.

Unfortunately, in the past, some school officials have resented the fact that the IDEA requires a manifestation determination and that students with disabilities cannot be expelled or suspended long term without school services. These officials may not know, or they may have forgotten, that for much of our history, children with disabilities were excluded entirely from the school system. Those who were not excluded often received minimal services.[198]

Some school officials have not been flexible or have had a zero tolerance or no exceptions approach to disciplining students with disabilities for violations of codes of student conduct. The IDEA 2004 affirmatively states that school personnel may consider any **unique circumstances on a case-by-case** basis when determining whether to order the change in placement of a student with a disability who violates a code of student conduct.[199] This provision might encourage flexibility, rather than a zero tolerance approach, to disciplining students with disabilities.

The authority of school personnel to remove a student for misconduct ordinarily is limited to short-term removals. However, school officials may extend a student's removal up to **45 school days** if the student's misconduct involves special circumstances. Note that, under the IDEA 2004, the extended removal is for **45 school days. Previously under the IDEA 97, the extended removal was for 45 calendar days**.

Special Circumstances

School personnel may remove a student with a disability to an alternative educational setting for not more than **45 school days** in cases involving special circumstances. **Note that**, for misconduct involving special circumstances, the student may be removed for not more than 45 school days regardless of whether the misconduct is determined to be a manifestation of the student's disability.[200] Special circumstances are cases where the student

1. Carries to or possesses a weapon at school, on school premises, or to or at a school function under the jurisdiction of a State or local education agency (note the school function does not have to be a function of the student's school district);

2. Knowingly possesses or uses illegal drugs, or sells or solicits the sale of a controlled substance, while at school, on school premises, or at a school function under the jurisdiction of a State or local education agency (again, **note** the function does not have to be a function of the student's school district); or

3. Has inflicted serious bodily injury upon another person while at school, on school premises, or at a school function under the jurisdiction of a State or local education agency (yes, again **note** the function doesn't have to be a function of the student's school district).[201]

"Weapon" is defined as "a device, instrument, material, or substance, animate or inanimate, that is used for or is readily capable of, causing death or serious bodily injury" with the exception that it "does not include a pocket knife with a blade of less than two and one-half inches."[202] Serious bodily injury "means bodily injury which involves a substantial risk of death, extreme physical pain, protracted and obvious disfigurement, or

---

[198] See the Congressional findings at 20 U.S.C. 1401(2)

[199] 20 U.S.C. 1415(k)(1)(A)

[200] 20 U.S.C. 1415(k)(1)(G)

[201] 20 U.S.C. 1415(k)(1)(G)(i)(ii)(iii)

[202] 18 U.S.C. 930(g)(2) Please note that school districts may have their own disciplinary policies with their own definition of "weapons" or other items that are banned from school. So, while the definition here defines when a student can be removed for an extended period of time that does not mean students can bring other items that might be prohibited by a code of student conduct to school.

protracted loss or impairment of the function of a bodily member, organ, or mental faculty."[203]

Under these special circumstances school officials, on their own, can remove the student for up to 45 school days. The removal must be to an interim alternative educational setting. **But the school district does not need to get the approval of a hearing officer**. To be sure, the student's parents can request a hearing if they disagree with the school district's determination regarding the interim setting or the existence of special circumstances, but the school district does not have to get a hearing officer's preapproval to take these actions.[204]

Again, if special circumstances exist, school officials can remove the student for up to 45 school days, whether or not the behavior was determined to be a manifestation of the student's disability. The student must receive educational services during this removal time. These services are in an interim alternative educational setting; that setting is determined by the IEP team.[205]

Manifestation Determination

The manifestation determination is the process used to determine whether the student's be-

> The manifestation determination is the process used to determine whether the student's behavior (perceived misconduct) is related to the student's disability. The manifestation determination is made to avoid punishing students for behavior that is disability related.

[203] 18 U.S.C. 1365(h)(3)
[204] 20 U.S.C. 1415(k)(1)(G) and (3)(A)
[205] 20 U.S.C. 1415(k)(1)(G) and (2)

havior (perceived misconduct) is related to the student's disability. The manifestation determination is made to avoid punishing students for behavior that is disability related.

The school district is required to conduct a meeting to make a manifestation determination any time the school district intends to remove the student beyond 10 school days. Removing a student with a disability beyond 10 school days is considered a change in placement; a change in placement requires a manifestation determination. A change in placement may require a functional behavioral assessment, and behavioral services and modifications that are designed to address the behavior so that the behavior does not happen again.

Also, remember that while the student can be removed without services for 10 school days, the student must receive services (in an interim alternative educational setting) if he is removed beyond 10 school days.

The Manifestation Determination Process

After deciding to remove a student for longer than 10 school days, the district has **10 school days** to hold a meeting to make a manifestation determination. The manifestation determination meeting does not necessarily require the entire IEP team. The IDEA 2004 says that determination is made by the parent, school district and **relevant members** of the IEP team. The student's parents and the school district decide which members of the IEP team are relevant and to be included in the manifestation determination meeting.

As noted in Chapter IV, at the parents' or school district's discretion, "other individuals who have knowledge or special expertise regarding the child including related services personnel" can be included as members of the IEP team.[206] Parents may want to invite private related service providers (such as psychologists, speech therapists, occupational therapists, or physical therapists) to the manifestation determination meeting as "relevant" members of the IEP team.

The manifestation determination team (school district representatives, parents, and relevant IEP team members) must review all pertinent information in the student's file. This review will include the student's IEP, teacher observations, and information provided by the student's parents. Based on that review, the team will determine

1. if the conduct in question was caused by, or had a direct and substantial relationship to, the student's disability; or

2. if the conduct in question was the direct result of the local education agency's failure to implement the IEP.

If the school district, the parent and relevant IEP team members determine that either (1) or (2) applies to the student, the misconduct will be determined to be a manifestation of the student's disability.[207]

If the Behavior Is a Manifestation of the Student's Disability

If the conduct is determined to be a manifestation of the student's disability, the **entire IEP team** will meet. The IEP team will take the following steps:

1. Conduct a functional behavioral assessment (FBA) and implement a behavioral intervention plan (BIP) for the student, unless the school district has already done a functional behavioral

assessment before the misconduct occurred. In that case, the team must review the adequacy of the assessment in light of the current situation.

2. If a behavioral intervention plan has already been developed, the team will review the plan and modify it as necessary to address the student's behavior.

3. Unless there are special circumstances, the IEP team will return the student to his current educational placement (the placement the student was in before the removal). The school district and the parents, however, may agree to change the student's current educational placement as part of modifying the behavioral intervention plan.[208]

If the Behavior Is Determined NOT to Be a Manifestation of the Student's Disability

If the student's behavior is not a manifestation of the student's disability, then the student may be disciplined the same as a student without a disability would be disciplined for the same misconduct. However, the student with a disability must continue to receive a free appropriate public education. These educational services must enable the student to continue to participate in the general

---

[206] 20 U.S.C. 1414(d)(1)(B)(vi)

[207] 20 U.S.C. 1415(k)(1)(E)(i)(ii) Note that this is a change from the IDEA 97. Under the IDEA 97 the manifestation determination was made by the IEP team and other qualified individuals and the IEP team looked at three issues, stated generally: (1) In relation to the student's behavior, was the placement appropriate, and IEP services delivered; (2) Did the student's disability impair the student's ability to understand the impact and consequences of the student's behavior; or (3) Did the student's disability impair the student's ability to control his behavior?

[208] 20 U.S.C. 1415(k)(1)(F)

> The interim alternative educational setting is determined by the IEP team. While in an interim alternative educational setting, the student must receive educational services that will enable the student to continue to participate in the general education curriculum, and to progress toward meeting the goals in his IEP.

education curriculum and to progress towards meeting the student's IEP goals. That education may be provided in an alternative educational setting.[209] Again, the services and educational setting are determined by the IEP team.[210]

Interim Alternative Educational Setting

If a student is removed for more than 10 school days, the student must receive educational services. In most cases those services will be delivered in an interim alternative educational setting (IAES).

As we have discussed, the student may be removed for more than 10 school days if (1) special circumstances exist (possession of weapons or drugs, or serious bodily injury inflicted on another), or (2) the student's misconduct is determined NOT to be a manifestation of the student's disability and school personnel want to remove the student for more than 10 school days because that is the discipline that would be applied to students without disabilities for similar violations of the student code of conduct.

[209] 20 U.S.C. 1415(k)(1)(C)(D)
[210] 20 U.S.C. 1415(k)(2)
[211] 20 U.S.C. 1415(k)(1)(H)
[212] 20 U.S.C. 1415(k)(1)(C)(D) and (2)
[213] 20 U.S.C. 1415(k)(3)(A)

The interim alternative educational setting is determined by the IEP team. While in an interim alternative educational setting, the student must receive educational services that will enable the student to continue to participate in the general education curriculum, and to progress toward meeting the goals in his IEP.

Additionally, the student should receive, as appropriate, a functional behavioral assessment (FBA) and behavioral intervention services and modifications that are designed to address the behavior so that it does not recur.[211]

Appeals and Procedural Safeguards

Notice

When the school district decides to take a disciplinary action regarding a student with a disability, the school district must notify the student's parents. The notice must be provided to the parents no later than the date the decision to take disciplinary action is made. The parents must be notified of all the procedural safeguards provided to students with disabilities in the disciplinary process.[212]

Disciplinary Appeal Process

When parents disagree with the decision that their child's behavior is not a manifestation of the child's disability, or the parents disagree with any decision regarding their child's placement during the disciplinary process, parents may request a hearing.[213] For example, parents may not like the interim alternative education setting. They may not think the alternative setting will allow the student to continue to progress in the general curriculum, or they may not think the interim setting allows the student to progress toward meeting the goals in the student's

IEP. Moreover, parents may disagree regarding whether or not it is appropriate to conduct a functional behavioral assessment, or they may disagree that the behavior intervention services and modifications are designed to address the behavior so that is doesn't happen again.

The school district also has the right to request a hearing. For example, the district may request a hearing if it believes that maintaining the student in the current placement is "substantially likely to result in injury to the child or to others. . ."[214]

Expedited Hearings and the Authority of the Hearing Officer

Expedited Hearing Timeline

Under the IDEA 2004, hearings regarding the above disciplinary issues are **expedited hearings**. Expedited means accelerated or sped up. Thus expedited hearings occur on a quicker schedule than the more customary hearings discussed in Chapter V, **Resolving Disputes under the IDEA**. Expedited hearings must occur within **20 school days** of the date the hearing is requested. Additionally, the hearing officer must make a decision within **10 school days** after the hearing.[215]

Authority of the Hearing Officer

After hearing the issues, the hearing officer may order a change in placement for the student. In ordering that change in placement, the hearing officer may (1) return the student to the student's current placement (the setting the student was in before the student was removed), or (2) order that the student's placement be changed to an interim alternative educational setting. The change in placement to the interim alternative educational setting may not be

for more than **45 school days**. To change the placement, the hearing officer must determine that "maintaining the student in the current placement is substantially likely to result in injury to the student or others."[216]

Placement during Disciplinary Appeals

The previous chapter regarding resolving disputes stated that students with disabilities ordinarily stay-put in their current educational program during an appeal. This is **not** the case during appeals that are made in the disciplinary process.

During an appeal of a disciplinary placement decision, the student will remain in the **interim alternative educational setting**. The student will remain in that setting until either (1) the hearing officer makes a decision, or (2) the time period that would apply to students without disabilities expires, whichever comes first.

Remember if the student's misconduct is determined **not** to be a manifestation of the student's disability, that student will be disciplined as students without disabilities would be disciplined.

What About Children Who Haven't Been Determined Eligible for Special Education?

The central question is "Did the school district know the student had a disability before the student misbehaved?" A student who has **not** been determined eligible for special education services has the protections provided in the disciplinary process if the school district

---

[214] 20 U.S.C. 1415(k)(3)(A)
[215] 20 U.S.C. 1415(k)(4)(B)
[216] 20 U.S.C. 1415(k)(3)(B)(ii)

> A student who has not been determined eligible for special education services has the protections provided in the disciplinary process if the school district had knowledge that the student had a disability before the behavior causing the disciplinary removal occurred.

had knowledge that the student had a disability before the behavior causing the disciplinary removal occurred.[217]

The IDEA 2004 considers that a school district has knowledge that the student has a disability if

1. the student's parent has expressed concern in writing to **supervisory or administrative personnel** or a teacher that the student needs special education and related services;

2. the parent has asked for an evaluation to determine if the student has a disability; or

3. the student's teacher or other school district personnel have expressed **specific concerns about a pattern of behavior demonstrated by the child, directly** to the director of special education of the school district or to other school district

supervisory personnel.[218]

If the school district knew that the student had a disability before the behavior causing the student's removal occurred, that student is considered to be a student with a disability in the disciplinary process. Consequently, the protections in the disciplinary process for students with disabilities will apply to this student.

What Happens If the School District Does NOT Know the Student Has a Disability?

The school district is NOT considered to have knowledge that the student has a disability (1) if the student's parents have not allowed the student to be evaluated for eligibility for special education services, or (2) the student's parents have refused special education services under the IDEA, or (3) the student has already been evaluated and it was determined the student was not eligible for special education services.[219]

If the school district does not know the student has a disability, the student may be disciplined the same as a student without disabilities would be disciplined for similar behavior.

What If the Parent Requests that the Student Be Evaluated after the Student Is in the Disciplinary Process?

When the student is in the disciplinary process and the parent requests an evaluation to determine whether the student is eligible for special education services, the school district must evaluate the student. Moreover, the evaluation must be expedited. While the evaluation is being conducted, the student will remain in the educational placement that has been determined by school authorities.

Essentially, the student is treated as a student without a disability during the evaluation pro-

---

[217] 20 U.S.C. 1415(k)(5)(A)

[218] 20 U.S.C. 1415(k)(5)(B) Note that under the IDEA 97 the school district was also deemed to have knowledge that the student had a disability if the behavior or "performance" of the student demonstrated the student needed special education services. Under the IDEA 2004 "performance" is no longer an expressed factor.

[219] 20 U.S.C. 1415(k)(5)(C)

cess. If the evaluation determines that, in fact, the student is eligible for special education services, then those services must be provided. Moreover, the student will be protected as a student with a disability in the disciplinary process.[220]

What To Do If Your Child Is Suspended

If you are notified that your son or daughter is being suspended or removed from the current placement, don't panic. Obviously, that's easier said than done. But it's still good advice.

Once the initial alarm has subsided, get the facts. What is the suspension for? How long is it for? Where will your child be during the suspension? Has the child been suspended for similar behavior before? If you need answers to these questions, call the school. Try your best not to get angry with school staff. As we discussed in the previous chapter, angry parents sometimes are discounted. Once you have all the information, put it together with what you have read in this chapter.

Is the removal for longer than 10 school days? If so, it is a change in placement. You know, therefore, that there will need to be a meeting to make a manifestation determination. You also know that if your child is removed for more than 10 school days, he must continue to receive educational services. Those services will be in an interim alternative educational setting. That means the IEP team will need to meet to develop the interim alternative educational setting. If the suspension is a change in placement, you should be told, at the time the child is suspended, about your procedural safeguards. Whatever is decided, you have the right to appeal.

If the suspension is not for more than 10 school days (a change in placement), you may still want to request an IEP meeting to discuss your child's behavior and his educational program. As we discussed in the chapter on the IEP process, IEP meetings are an excellent tool for clarifying issues and resolving disputes. At the IEP meeting, you can participate in the discussion regarding the need for a functional behavioral assessment, selecting an interim alternative educational setting, and the manifestation determination.

If you are unclear about the facts or the process, call the school. If you are still unclear, or the information sounds inaccurate, call the director of special education. You might also call the State Education Agency for information about the disciplinary process. The disciplinary process for students with disabilities is sometimes misunderstood and sometimes misapplied. Unfortunately, general educators are sometimes not as aware of this process as they might be. Parents, therefore, should follow up on information that sounds incorrect with special education personnel.

Many parents mistakenly leap to the conclusion that suspension means their child will be expelled without school services. In fact, most often, the student is not expelled. Remember, the student cannot be punished or expelled for conduct that is a manifestation of the student's disability. Indeed, IEP teams frequently determine that the student's conduct is a manifestation of the student's disability. Also remember that students with disabilities, including students who are long-term suspended or expelled, must be provided a free appropriate public education.

---

[220] 20 U.S.C. 1415(k)(5)(D)

Notes:

VII Children in Private Schools

Some students with disabilities attend private, rather than public schools. There are three reasons a student with a disability might be enrolled in a private school. First, the public school, through the IEP team, might place a student with a disability in a private school to get a free appropriate public education. Second, the student's parents might disagree that the public school system can meet their child's educational needs, so the parents enroll the student in a private program. Third, the parents simply want a private school and choose to place their child in a private school.

The IDEA specifically addresses each of these situations. In this chapter, I will discuss the IDEA and services for children with disabilities who attend private schools. Additionally, private schools may not discriminate against children with disabilities under the Americans with Disabilities Act (ADA). I will discuss the Americans with Disabilities Act in the next chapter. First, let's look at what the IDEA requires.

Private School Placements by the Public Schools

The IEP team might place a student with disabilities in a private school to receive an appropriate education. In that case, the student is entitled to the same rights and services the student would receive if the student was placed

> The IEP team might place a student with disabilities in a private school to receive an appropriate education. In that case, the student is entitled to the same rights and services the student would receive if the student was placed in a public school.

in a public school. The IDEA refers to these circumstances as the child being "placed in or referred to such schools or facilities [private schools] by the State or appropriate local education agency as a means of carrying out the requirements of. . ." the IDEA.[221]

Before placing a student in a private program, the school district must have an IEP meeting. Additionally, the district must ensure that a representative of the private school participates in the meeting. If the representative cannot attend the meeting, the district should use other methods, such as conference calls, to ensure participation.

After a student enters the private school, IEP meetings may be initiated and conducted by the private school. But the school district must still make sure that the student's parents and a school district representative are involved in the meetings. In particular, the parents and public school representative must agree to any proposed changes in the student's IEP before those changes are implemented.[222]

Private School Placements by Parents Because the Public School Program Is Inappropriate

Parents may not agree that the public school has offered an appropriate program for their child. Consequently, these parents enroll their child in a private program to get the services the parents believe the child should have received from the public schools. The public schools, however, did not place the student in a private program in order to get a free appropriate public education under the IDEA. Under certain circumstances, these parents may be entitled to

Congress wanted the public schools to have a chance to fix the problem before the student was enrolled privately. Consequently, the IDEA requires that parents, before removing their child, tell the school district that they are rejecting the public placement and enrolling their child in a private program at public expense.

be reimbursed, by the public schools, for the tuition they paid to the private program.

This tuition reimbursement may be obtained through a court or hearing officer, if the parents establish two key points: (1) the program offered by the public school, before the student was enrolled in the private school, was inappropriate, and (2) the private program was, in fact, appropriate.[223] The parents can establish these points through the due process hearing procedures.

However, there are circumstances in which, despite the establishment of those two key points, the amount of tuition the parents would have been reimbursed may be reduced or denied. In reauthorizing the IDEA, Congress wanted parents to be able to obtain tuition reimbursement if the public schools failed to offer appropriate programs. But Congress also wanted school districts to be notified that parents were dissatisfied with the public school program and intended to enroll their child in a private program.

Congress wanted the public schools to have a chance to fix the problem before the student was enrolled privately. Consequently, the IDEA requires that parents, before removing their child, tell the school district that they are

---

[221] 20 U.S.C. 1412(a)(10)(B)
[222] 20 U.S.C. 1412(a)(10)(B)
[223] 20 U.S.C. 1412(a)(10)(C)

rejecting the public placement and enrolling their child in a private program at public expense. The parents must also tell the school district their concerns about the public placement.

The parents may inform the school district that they are enrolling their child in a private school in two ways: (1) the parents may tell the district about their concerns at the most recent IEP meeting the parents attend before removing their child from the public school, or (2) the parents may provide this information in writing. If the second option is taken, the written notification must be provided to the school district at least 10 business days before the student is removed from the public school.

The amount of tuition reimbursed to parents may also be reduced or denied if the school district proposed to evaluate the student before the student was removed from the public school, but the parents didn't make the student available for the evaluation, or if the court determines the parents acted unreasonably.[224]

Students Whose Parents Choose Private School Placement

Some families voluntarily choose to enroll their children in private schools. The IDEA refers to these children as "being enrolled in private schools by their parents" or "parentally placed private school children."[225] These private school students are entitled to some services from the public schools, but they are not entitled to the same services they would receive if enrolled in a public school program or placed in the private program by the public schools. Generally, the IDEA tries to ensure that school districts provide a fair or equitable share of IDEA funds to support

services to parentally placed private school children with disabilities.

Child Find

School districts are required to locate, identify, and evaluate all private school children with disabilities, including religious school children, who live in the district. This child find obligation is the same for private school children as it is for public school children.[226]

> School districts are required to locate, identify, and evaluate all private school children with disabilities, including religious school children, who live in the district. This child find obligation is the same for private school children as it is for public school children.

Moreover, the child find process must be designed to ensure equitable participation of students who are placed by their parents in private schools, and the process must be designed to get an accurate count of these children.[227] Beyond child find, however, the public school obligation for private school children with disabilities is different from their obligation to students enrolled in public school programs.

Service Coordination and Planning

As noted earlier, generally, the IDEA tries to ensure that school districts provide a fair or equitable share (proportion) of IDEA funds to sup-

---

[224] 20 U.S.C. 1412(a)(10)(C)
[225] 20 U.S.C. 1412(a)(10)(A)
[226] 20 U.S.C. 1412(a)(10)
[227] 20 U.S.C. 1412(a)(10)(A)(ii)

port services to parentally placed private school children with disabilities. The IDEA states this concept in this way: "To the extent consistent with the number and location of children with disabilities in the state who are enrolled by their parents in private elementary schools and secondary schools in the school district served by a local education agency, provision is made for the participation of those children in the program assisted or carried out by this part. . ."[228]

Again, the IDEA is trying to ensure these students have access to their fair share or proportion of IDEA funds. Thus, the IDEA lays out a process for states and school districts to determine that proportion and a process to determine how to plan to deliver services to parentally placed private students with disabilities.

To determine how to serve parentally placed private school children, the school district and the State Education Agency, where appropriate, must consult with private school representatives and representatives of the parents. The consultation should include

1. the child find process and how these children can participate equitably;

2. the determination of the proportionate amount of federal funds available for these students, and how the amount was calculated;

3. how the consultation process between the school district, the representative of private schools, and the representatives of parents of parentally placed private school children will work;

4. how, where, and by whom special education services will be provided for these students; and

5. how, if the district and private school officials disagree, the school district will provide a written explanation to private school officials of the reasons why the district chose not to provide services.[229]

Finally, the IDEA 2004 provides a complaint process for private school officials to complain to the State Education Agency if they believe the consultation process with the school district was not meaningful, timely, or didn't adequately consider the private school official's views.[230]

Services Plans for Parentally-placed Private School Children with Disabilities

Parentally-placed private school students do not have an individual right to receive the same or all of the special education and related services the students would receive if enrolled in public school.[231] In fact, the amount school districts must spend on providing services to private school children is limited. For parentally-placed private school children the public schools are only required to spend an amount proportionate to the number of private school children with disabilities compared to the number of public school children with disabilities. This proportion is determined, district by district, based on the number of students with disabilities living in each district. To determine how the district will spend that allocation, school districts must consult with representatives of private schools within their districts.

If a student with a disability is enrolled in a private school, but will receive special education services from the school district, then the

[228] 20 U.S.C. 1412(a)(10)(A)(i)
[229] 20 U.S.C. 1412(a)(10)(A)(iii)
[230] 20 U.S.C. 1412(a)(10)(A)(v)
[231] 34 CFR 300.137

district must develop a *services plan* for the student.[232] A *services plan* is similar to an IEP, but developed specifically for students in private schools who receive special education services from the public school district. The plan must specifically describe the special education and related services the private school student will receive from the school district. In developing this plan, however, private school children may receive a different amount of services than students in the public schools. The services are provided based upon the school district's allocation of funds for private school children and the plan the district has developed, in consultation with private school representatives, to serve private school children.

Services to private school children may be provided at the public school, at a service site, or at the private school. A service site is a place where the student receives services that is not the public school or private school. For example, a service site might be a community library or other community center where the student might receive services. If a student requires transportation, to benefit from the special education services being provided, then transportation must be provided. But the school district is **not** required to transport students from their home to the private school or from the private school to their home. Transportation can be provided from the student's home to a service site, or from the student's home to the student's public school.[233]

Appeal Process for Parentally-Placed Private School Children

Parents who choose to enroll their children in private schools do not have the same due process procedures available to them as parents of children in the public schools. Private school parents may not use the due process hearing procedures to appeal the services plan or the district's failure to comply with the service plan. Those issues can be taken to the State Education Agency through the State Education Agency Complaint Process discussed in Chapter V.[234] Parents of private school children, however, may use the due process hearing procedures to appeal issues regarding the district's child find obligation to locate, identify, and evaluate children with disabilities.

Notes:

---

[232] 34 CFR 300.138
[233] 34 CFR 300.139
[234] 34 CFR 300.140

Notes:

VIII

Section 504 of the Rehabilitation Act of 1973 and the Americans with Disabilities Act

Section 504 of the Rehabilitation Act of 1973, enacted before Congress passed the Education for All Handicapped Children Act, was the first major federal legislation protecting people with disabilities from discrimination. Congress passed Section 504 to protect persons with disabilities from discrimination from employers and service providers who receive support from the federal government.[235]

Section 504, therefore, requires that agencies and programs that receive federal funding provide equal access to the agency's services, programs, and activities. If an agency receives federal funding, it cannot discriminate against qualified persons with disabilities in any of its activities, including its employment practices. But employers, programs, agencies, and private

facilities that do not receive federal funding are not covered by Section 504. Thus, there was a gap in the coverage of federal law prohibiting discrimination against persons with disabilities.

To bridge that gap, Congress enacted the Americans with Disabilities Act (ADA) in 1990.[236] The ADA also protects qualified persons with disabilities from discrimination, but the ADA's requirements reach beyond employers, programs, agencies, and facilities that receive federal funding.

The ADA requires equal access for qualified persons with disabilities to employment, state and local governmental services and transportation, to goods and services provided by public accommodations, and to telephone and telecommunication services. Remember, unlike Section 504, the ADA does not require that an entity receive federal funding in order to be covered by the ADA.

[235] 29 U.S.C. 794
[236] 42 U.S.C. 12101-12213

Section 504 and the ADA protect both children and adults with disabilities. Section 504 applies to the public elementary and secondary education system and to the public higher education system because both systems receive federal funding. Like the IDEA, Section 504 requires that school districts provide students with disabilities a free appropriate public education.

Although the ADA applies to the public school system, it doesn't have a specific requirement that children with disabilities be provided a free appropriate public education. The Office for Civil Rights,

> An appropriate education under Section 504 means providing regular or special education and related services to meet the individual educational needs of children with disabilities as adequately as the needs of children without disabilities are met. Thus, Section 504 focuses on guaranteeing equal access to educational services for students with disabilities.

[237] *Manteca (CA) Unified School District*, 30 IDELR 544 (OCR 1998)
[238] For a discussion of differences between the IDEA and Section 504 see *OCR Senior Staff Memoranda* 14 EHLR 307:01 (Oct. 24, 1988)
[239] 34 C.F.R. Part 104.33(a)(b)
[240] See *Wisconsin (WI) Heights School District*, 30 IDELR 619 (OCR 1998), student with a mobility impairment needed a sanitary restroom near her classroom, and see *Santa Maria-Bonita (CA) School District*, 30 IDELR 547 (OCR1998), students with diabetes complained that district policy against carrying hypodermic "sharps" to class was discriminatory since it required students to leave class during instruction time to conduct blood glucose tests. After the complaint, the students were allowed to bring their diabetes kits with hypodermic "sharps" to school and conduct their own blood glucose tests while in class.

however, has interpreted Title II of the ADA to have the same requirement to provide a free appropriate public education as Section 504.[237]

Moreover, the definition of a person with a disability is broader under the ADA and Section 504 than the definition of a child with a disability under the IDEA. Likewise, the parameters of a free appropriate public education under Section 504 differ significantly from what constitutes a free appropriate public education under the IDEA.[238]

What Is a Free Appropriate Public Education under Section 504?

Section 504 requires that school districts provide a free appropriate public education to children with disabilities within their jurisdiction, regardless of the nature or severity of the student's disability. The term jurisdiction means the student is eligible for services from a particular district. For example, to be eligible for Section 504 protections from a particular district, the child or the child's parents may need to live within the district and the child must be of school age.

An appropriate education under Section 504 means providing regular or special education and related services to meet the individual educational needs of children with disabilities **as adequately as the needs of children without disabilities are met**.[239] Thus, section 504 focuses on guaranteeing equal access to educational services for students with disabilities.

This is a different focus than the free appropriate public education requirements of the IDEA. To meet the needs of students with disabilities as adequately as the needs of students without disabilities are met, Section 504 requires that school districts provide accommodations, special education and related and supplementary services to support the student with a disability.[240]

Those accommodations and special education and support services are determined through a meeting of the student's parents and appropriate general education staff at the school. These services are usually written into a **504 Plan** for the student. Although Section 504 doesn't specifically require a written plan like the IDEA's individualized educational program, most school districts will put the plan in writing. Unlike a student's IEP under the IDEA, the student's **504 Plan** is only required to include the services the student with a Section **504 disability** needs to make sure that the student's educational needs are met as well as the needs of students without disabilities are met.[241] School districts must provide the services and accommodations that are outlined in the 504 Plan.[242]

Like the IDEA, Section 504 addresses placing students with disabilities in the least restrictive environment. Section 504 requires that students with disabilities receive educational services with students without disabilities to the maximum extent appropriate to the needs of the student with a disability.

To put this into practice, Section 504 requires schools to teach students with disabilities in the regular educational environment, unless teaching the student in that regular setting, with the use of supplementary aids and services, cannot be achieved satisfactorily. When placing students with disabilities in settings other than the regular educational environment, the school district must consider how close the alternate setting is to the student's home.[243]

Furthermore, schools must make sure that students with disabilities participate in non-

academic and extracurricular activities with students without disabilities, to the maximum extent appropriate to the needs of the student with a disability. Included in nonacademic and extracurricular activities are meals, recess periods, counseling services, physical recreational athletics, transportation, health services, recreational activities, special interest groups or clubs, referrals to agencies that provide assistance to persons with disabilities, and employment of students.[244]

---

[241] *Kalama School District No. 402* 35 IDELR 72 (OCR 2000), school district had notice that two students had asthma that affected their ability to participate in school, but did not initiate and complete an evaluation and develop a 504 Plan with accommodations. District agreed to conduct comprehensive evaluations, provide 504 Plan and study student's need for compensatory services during year they were denied FAPE.

[242] *New Bedford Public Schools* 42 IDELR 208 (OCR 2004), 504 Plan for a student with a social emotional disability required placement in a classroom with a 6:1 student-teacher ratio, but district failed to place her in the classroom. Additionally, school district denied the student a free appropriate public education when it changed her placement without first convening a 504 team meeting.

[243] 34 C.F.R. Part 104.34(a)

[244] 34 C.F.R. Part 104.34(b) and 104.37(a) and see *Inskip v. Astoria Sch. District*, 30 IDELR 398 (D. Or. 1999), court ruled that a student with autism be allowed to play in softball games. School district had said that she was not qualified to play because her participation created a "reasonable probability of substantial injury". But see *Garden Grove Unified School District* 35 IDELR 227 (OCR 2001) although basketball coach treated student differently from other players, it wasn't due to her disability. All the players who were not starters were treated differently.

Who Is a Person with a Disability under 504?

As discussed earlier, Section 504 encompasses more than education in the public schools. Its definition of a person with a disability is, therefore, broader than the definition of a child with a disability under the IDEA. A person has a disability under section 504 if the individual has a physical or mental impairment that substantially limits one or more of the individual's major life activities.

Life activities are functions such as caring for one's self, performing manual tasks, walking, seeing, hearing, speaking, breathing, learning, and working. A person can also be protected if they have a record of having an impairment or are regarded as having an impairment.[245]

Generally, however, a person who is protected as a person with a disability because they have a record of an impairment or are regarded as having an impairment is not entitled to accommodations for that perception or record of impairment. A student, however, who is perceived as having a disability or has a record of having a disability is entitled to the 504 protections in the disciplinary process.[246]

Unlike the IDEA definition of a child with a disability, under Section 504 a child doesn't have to need special education and related services to have a disability. All that is required under Section 504 is that the child have an impairment that substantially limits a major life

function. There are children, therefore, who have impairments, but don't need special education services. They may not have disabilities under the IDEA, but they may have disabilities under Section 504, if they have impairments that substantially limit a major life function.

For example, a student with arthritis **may not** need special education services, and, therefore, would not have a disability under the IDEA. But it is likely that this student has a disability under Section 504. Very often, arthritis substantially limits a major life activity. The student would then be entitled to a **504 Plan** and those services that are needed to ensure that the student's needs are met to the same extent as the needs of students without disabilities.

Again, a child who has a disability under Section 504 is entitled to a free appropriate public education from the school district. An appropriate education under Section 504 would mean **the child is provided regular or special education and related aids and services that are designed to meet that student's individual educational needs as adequately as the needs of students without disabilities are met**.[247]

> A person has a disability under section 504 if the individual has a physical or mental impairment that substantially limits one or more of the individual's major life activities.

Examples of 504 Accommodations

- A student with an illness such as cancer may need a modified class schedule that allows for rest and recuperation following chemotherapy.

[245] 34 C.F.R. Part 104.3(j) and 104.37(a) See also *OCR Staff Memorandum* 16 IDELR 712 (OCR 1990) students with HIV/AIDS have a disability under Section 504.
[246] *Letter to Veir*, 20 IDELR 864 (OCR 1996)
[247] For discussion of 504 requirements see *Letter to Veir*, 20 IDELR 864 (OCR 1996).

- A student with a learning disability that affects the ability to demonstrate knowledge on a standardized test may require modified test arrangements such as oral testing, additional time for tests, etc.

- A student with a learning disability or a visual impairment may need a note-taker or tape recorder.

- A student with a chronic medical problem or physical impairment may have difficulty walking distances or climbing stairs and may need classes relocated, extra time between classes, a special parking place, or other accommodations.

- A student with mental illness may need a modified class schedule to allow time for regular counseling or therapy.

- A student with a seizure disorder and whose seizures are stimulated by stress may need an accommodation for stressful activities such as lengthy academic testing or competitive endeavors in physical education.

- A student with arthritis may require a modified or adaptive physical education program.

- A student with a disability that affected the ability to write may need access to a keyboard.

Evaluation under Section 504

The schools must evaluate students who are believed to have a 504 disability and need special education and related services. This must be done before the student is initially placed in regular or special education. An evaluation must also be done before the student's placement is changed. The tests that are used for evaluations under section 504 must be validated for the specific purposes for which they are used and administered by trained personnel. Moreover, the evaluation materials must be tailored to assess specific areas of educational need.

Finally, tests must be selected and administered so that when the test is given to a student with impaired sensory, manual, or speaking skills, the tests accurately reflect the student's aptitude or achievement level. Thus, the test should not reflect the student's impaired sensory, manual, or speaking skills unless those are the skills that are being measured.[248] The school district must also make sure that students are periodically re-evaluated. In particular, a student must be re-evaluated if the school district is considering significantly changing the student's placement.[249]

Once the evaluation process is completed decisions to place the student must be made by a group of persons. That group must include

> The schools must evaluate students who are believed to have a 504 disability and need special education and related services. This must be done before the student is initially placed in regular or special education. An evaluation must also be done before the student's placement is changed.

---

[248] 34 C.F.R. Part 104.35
[249] 34 C.F.R. Part 104.35(a) and see *New Bedford Public Schools*, 42 IDELR 208 (OCR 2004) School district changed student's placement without first convening a 504 team meeting.

persons knowledgeable about the student, the meaning of the evaluation data, and the placement options.[250]

Standardized Assessments

As you are aware, there is a national push for standardized assessments of student progress. Students with disabilities who need accommodations when taking tests should have those accommodations specifically noted in their 504 plans. An accommodation is a change made to the assessment procedures to provide a student with access to information and an equal opportunity to demonstrate knowledge and skills without affecting the reliability or validity of the assessment. An accommodation does not change the instructional level, content, or the performance criteria of the assessment.

Some examples of possible accommodations include extended time; administering the test in more, but shorter sessions; providing Braille or large print versions of the test; and providing assistive technology such as visual magnification devices, pencil grips, and noise buffers.

Accommodations must be content-area specific, and the student is entitled to use only those accommodations needed for the specific content area being assessed. Finally, students are allowed more than one accommodation. For example, a student using a Braille version of the test may also need extra time. Obviously, if a student requires accommodations when taking assessments, it is very important that the accommodations be documented on the student's 504 plan.

---

[250] 34 C.F.R. Part 104.36 and see *Manteca (CA) Unified School District* 30 IDELR 544 (OCR 1998), where the school district violated 504 because the placement decision was made by an individual resource specialist rather than a group of individuals.

Assistive Technology and Section 504

Students with disabilities are entitled to assistive technology devices and services under Section 504 if the student needs those services to ensure equal access to the public school program. Remember, under Section 504, the needs of students with disabilities must be met as well as the needs of students without disabilities are met. The school district must provide related services and supplementary aids and services to meet that requirement.

Assistive technology services are included as supplementary aids and services or related services under Section 504. For example, if a student with a physical disability couldn't sit at a regular desk, Section 504 might require provision of a specially designed desk. A student with arthritis might be provided with an assistive device to help the student write, or a student who could not physically write might be provided with a word processor and keyboard. Similarly, a student with a learning disability might need access to a keyboard and to "spell check" through a computer in order to write legibly and correctly.

Any type of assistive technology device or service may possibly be obtained under Section 504 if the device or service is needed to ensure equal participation in the public school program for the student with a disability. Re-

> Students with disabilities are entitled to assistive technology devices and services under Section 504 if the student needs those services to ensure equal access to the public school program.

lated or supplementary aids and services must be provided to support students in the regular educational environment. In fact, a school district must consider providing related or supplementary aids and services before the district removes the student from the regular educational setting. Assistive technology services can, therefore, be required under section 504 to ensure a student's participation in the regular educational environment.

Discipline and 504

Just as with the IDEA, Section 504 prohibits schools from punishing students for misconduct that is related to their disability.[251] Thus, Section 504 also requires that the school have a meeting to determine if the student's misconduct was a manifestation of the student's disability. Similar to the IDEA process, this manifestation meeting is triggered if the school is proposing excluding him indefinitely (expulsion), or for more than 10 consecutive school days, or if there is a pattern of excluding the student from school.[252]

Excluding the student from school for more than 10 consecutive school days is a significant change in placement. Under 504, a significant change in placement requires that the school conduct a re-evaluation.[253] A first step in this re-evaluation is determining whether the student's disability caused the misconduct. Additionally, a series of suspensions in a school year that are each less than 10 consecutive school days may also be considered a significant change in placement if it constitutes a "pattern of exclusion."

A pattern of exclusion is determined on a case by case basis. Factors to be considered in determining a pattern of exclusion are the length of each suspension, the proximity of the sus-

pensions to one another, and the total amount of time the student is excluded from school. The Office for Civil Rights (OCR) will not consider a series of suspensions that total less than 10 days in a school year to be a significant change in placement. But, OCR will consider a series of suspensions that total more than 10 days in a school year to be a significant change in placement requiring a re-evaluation and a manifestation determination meeting.

This manifestation determination meeting would include the parents of the student and other individuals who can contribute information regarding the student. If the student's misconduct is related to the student's disability, then the student may not be continually suspended or expelled for that conduct. The Office for Civil Rights has stated there are two circumstances in which a student with a disability may be suspended even though the behavior is determined

> Just as with the IDEA, Section 504 prohibits schools from punishing students for misconduct that is related to their disability. Thus, Section 504 also requires that the school have a meeting to determine if the student's misconduct was a manifestation of the student's disability.

[251] See *S-1 v. Turlington,* 635 F. 2d 342 (5th Cir. 1981)
[252] *Shelby County School District* 35 IDELR 228 (OCR 2001) preschool student expelled from YMCA program providing services under contract with the district for behavior related to disability. *Tustin Unified School District* 31 IDELR 139 (OCR 1999) Student with 504 disability engaged in illegal use of drugs at school not entitled to manifestation determination under 504 prior to expulsion.
[253] 34 C.F.R. 104.35(a)

to be a manifestation of the student's disability: (1) genuine emergencies; or (2) if the district is meeting in order to revise the student's IEP to deal with the discipline problem.[254]

Unlike the IDEA, however, Section 504 allows that if the student's disability is not related to the misconduct, then the student may be disciplined in the same manner as any other student, including being suspended or expelled **without services**.

Remember that section 504 prohibits discrimination against students with disabilities. This means students with 504 disabilities may be disciplined the same as students without disabilities are disciplined, so long as they are not punished for conduct that is related to their disability.[255] Finally, parents and students with disabilities have procedural safeguards under Section 504 and can appeal decisions made by the school district.[256]

---

[254] *OCR Memorandum* 307 IDELR 07 (OCR 1989)

[255] For a general discussion of Section 504 and student discipline see *Senior Staff Memorandum* regarding Long–term Suspension or Expulsion of Handicapped Students, 14 EHLR 307:05 (Oct. 28, 1988).

[256] *Forest Hills Public School District*, 42 IDELR 210 (OCR 2004) The school district violated Section 504 because it did not implement a system of procedural safeguards and did not inform a parent that she had the right a hearing to appeal a manifestation determination.

[257] 34 C.F.R. Part 104.36 and see *Manteca (CA) Unified School District* 30 IDELR 544 (OCR 1998) School district failed to inform of their right to appeal a denial of eligibility.

[258] *Ann Arbor Public Schools* 35 IDELR 279 (OCR2001) Parents with visual impairments entitled to Braille copies of IEPs, parent handbook, model for filing due process requests, and information about free or low-cost legal services.

Procedural Safeguards under Section 504

Like the IDEA, Section 504 gives parents procedural safeguards. Parents have the right to examine their child's educational records, the right to notice, and the right to an impartial hearing. Parents have the right to appeal actions by the school district regarding the identification, evaluation, or educational placement of the student. Parents and guardians have the right to be present at the hearing and the right to be represented by an attorney. There is also the right to have the results of the impartial hearing reviewed.[257]

Although parents should be informed by the school district about these procedures, it would be wise to specifically request them from the district if a parent has Section 504 concerns. Section 504 compliance is a general education responsibility rather than a special education responsibility. Unfortunately, many general educators are not as aware as they might be of its requirements. But each school district is required to have Section 504 procedures.[258] Again, it would be wise to ask for these specific procedures if seeking 504 services is a possibility.

The Americans with Disabilities Act

The Americans with Disabilities Act (ADA) also prohibits discrimination against qualified persons with disabilities. The ADA has four titles, or parts, that prohibit discrimination by various sectors of our society against qualified persons with disabilities.

Title I prohibits employment discrimination by employers with 15 or more employees. Title II prohibits discrimination in employment or access to governmental services by state and local governmental entities. Title III prohibits discrimination by public accommodations. Public accommodations include a wide range of entities that provide goods and services to the public. But Title III does not apply to public accommodations that are operated by private clubs and religious entities.

Finally, Title IV applies to the telecommunications industry. Title IV requires that telephone companies provide relay services by which individuals with communication impairments can make phone calls. A relay service allows a person who has a hearing impairment and uses a telecommunication device for the deaf (TDD) to send a typed message to an operator who will make a voice "relay" of the call on behalf of the person with the disability.

As we noted earlier, unlike Section 504, the ADA does not require that agencies receive federal funding to be covered. But the definition of an individual with a disability, under the ADA, is generally the same as the definition under Section 504.

Since school districts and school boards are local governmental entities, they are covered by Title II of the ADA. Like Section 504, Title II prohibits discrimination against students with disabilities, but Title II does not have the specific requirement that school districts provide students with disabilities a free appropriate public education.

Title II itself, therefore, does not have the extensive requirements contained in the Section 504 regulations regarding providing a free appropriate public education (such as meeting the individual educational needs of the student with a disability, evaluation and placement procedures, and procedural safeguards).

As noted earlier, however, the Office for Civil Rights has interpreted Title II to have the same requirements for school districts regarding providing a free appropriate public education as Section 504.

Title II specifically requires that school districts provide auxiliary aids and services that would be needed to ensure effective communication for persons with disabilities in using the school district's services.[259]

Included in examples of auxiliary aids and services are such assistive technology devices as telephone handset amplifiers, assistive listening devices, assistive listening systems, telephones compatible with hearing aids, closed captioned decoders, taped texts, audio recordings, Brailled materials, and large print materials.[260]

Finally, the Office for Civil Rights within the United States Department of Education administratively enforces both Section 504 and the ADA as they pertain to school districts.

Title III and Private Schools

Title III of the ADA applies to privately operated public accommodations. Included in the listing of public accommodations are places of

> As we noted earlier, unlike Section 504, the ADA does not require that agencies receive federal funding to be covered. But the definition of an individual with a disability, under the ADA, is generally the same as the definition under Section 504.

[259] 28 C.F.R. 35.130(f)
[260] 28 C.F.R. 35.104(1) and (2)

education and elementary and secondary private schools.[261] Private schools, therefore, are prohibited from discriminating against qualified students with disabilities.[262] But Title III does not specifically require that private schools provide an appropriate education to students with disabilities.

While students with disabilities who choose to attend private schools may not have the right to an appropriate education from the private school, private school students do have the right to receive auxiliary aids and services that are needed to ensure equal access to the school's educational program. Private schools are required to make sure that individuals with disabilities are not denied services, segregated, or treated differently because of the absence of auxiliary aids and services.[263]

Included in the definition of auxiliary aids and services are assistive technology devices like computer-aided transcription services, telephone handset amplifiers, assistive listening devices, telephones compatible with hearing aids, closed captioned decoders, open and closed captioning, TDDs, and videotext displays.[264]

Private schools must also assess the architectural and communication barriers that currently exist within their facilities. The school must remove those barriers if their removal is readily achievable. Readily achievable means the barrier can be removed without significant difficulty or expense. New construction built by the private school and alterations done in existing buildings must be accessible.

If a private school is required to provide a service as an auxiliary aid or service, the school may not impose a surcharge on the individual with a disability or their family for the cost of the aid or service.[265]

The obligation to provide these services, however, is not unlimited. Private schools are not required to provide an auxiliary aid or service if the school can show how providing the service would fundamentally alter their program or require significant difficulty or expense.[266] Also, not all private schools are covered by Title III. The ADA does not cover private schools that are operated by religious entities.[267] Religious entities are religious organizations or entities that are controlled by religious organizations.[268]

Finally, Title III of the ADA is administratively enforced by the United States Department of Justice. The Department of Justice

---

[261] 42 U.S.C. 12181(7)(j)

[262] See *Thomas v. Davidson Academy*, 846 F. Supp. 611, 20 IDELR 1375 (M.D. Tenn. 1994), private school that was covered by 504 and ADA could not expel student with a serious autoimmune disease who shouted expletives after cutting herself during art class. An expert in treating children with blood diseases testified that an exaggerated reaction was to be expected from the student who thought she might bleed to death.

[263] 28 C.F.R. 36.303

[264] 28 C.F.R. 36.303(b)

[265] 28 C.F.R. 36.301(c)

[266] 28 C.F.R. 36.303

[267] 28 C.F.R. 36.102(e)

[268] 28 C.F.R. 36.104

> Included in the listing of public accommodations are places of education and elementary and secondary private schools. Private schools, therefore, are prohibited from discriminating against qualified students with disabilities.

also has a mediation project to help resolve disputes under Titles II and III.

Disability Harassment

Disability harassment violates both Section 504 and the ADA. Disability harassment is intimidation or abusive behavior toward a student that creates a hostile environment by interfering with or denying the student's participation in or receipt of benefits, services, or opportunities in the school's program.[269]

Harassing conduct may include verbal acts like name-calling, and nonverbal acts such as drawn or written statements, or conduct that is physically threatening, harmful, or humiliating. To prevent or respond to disability harassment, schools and school districts are responsible for controlling the acts and behavior of other students, as well as the behavior of teachers and other employees. The Office for Civil Rights has provided the following as examples of disability harassment.[270]

- Several students continually remark out loud to other students during class that a student with a disability is "retarded" or "deaf and dumb" and does not belong in the class; as a result, the harassed student has difficulty doing work in class and her grades decline.[271]

- A student repeatedly places classroom furniture or other objects in the path of classmates who use wheelchairs, impeding the classmates' ability to enter the classroom.

- Students continually taunt or belittle a student with mental retardation by mocking and intimidating him so he does not participate in class.

- A school administrator repeatedly denies a student with a disability access to lunch, field trips, assemblies, and extra-curricular activities as a punishment for taking time off from school for required services related to the student's disability.

- A professor repeatedly belittles and criticizes a student with a disability for using accommodations in class, with the result that the student is so discouraged that she has difficulty performing in the class and learning.

> Disability harassment violates both Section 504 and the ADA. Disability harassment is intimidation or abusive behavior toward a student that creates a hostile environment by interfering with or denying the student's participation in or receipt of benefits, services, or opportunities in the school's program.

---

[269] *Letter to Colleague from Norma Cantu*, Asst. Secretary for Civil Rights and Judith Heuman, Asst. Secretary Office of Special Education and Rehabilitation Services, July 26, 2000. This letter is in Appendix C.

[270] July 26, 2000 *Letter to Colleague*, pages 3 and 4.

[271] See *Manteca (CA) Unified School District*, 30 IDELR 544 (OCR 1998), other students called student with ADD and OCD "crazy"; the student became depressed, had anorexia; as a result, her psychiatrist recommended she be removed from school and placed on home study. OCR found that the school district failed to investigate whether a hostile environment existed regarding the student with a disability.

Schools, school districts, colleges and universities have a legal responsibility under 504 and Title II of the ADA to prevent and respond to disability harassment. To prevent disability harassment, educational institutions must establish grievance procedures that can be used to address disability harassment.

Retaliation

Sometimes individuals are intimidated or harassed because they are trying to enforce or take advantage of their rights under Section 504 or the Americans with Disabilities Act (ADA). Section 504 and the ADA prohibit retaliation against a person with disabilities and persons acting on their behalf for trying to enforce their rights under these civil rights laws.[272] The anti-retaliation provisions of Section 504 and the ADA are very broad. It is a violation of 504 and the ADA to intimidate, threaten, coerce, or discriminate against an individual because the individual has engaged in a "protected activity." Protected activities include filing a complaint, testifying, assisting in, or participating in an investigation or hearing under 504 or the ADA.

The key elements in a complaint for retaliation are

1. the person making the retaliation claim engaged in a "protective activity" (they asserted a right, filed a complaint, testified, assisted or participated in an investigation or hearing under 504 or the ADA);

2. the school district knew the person engaged in a "protected activity" (asserted the right, filed the complaint, testified in a hearing, etc);

3. the school district took some action against the individual making the complaint and the action was at the same time or after the individual engaged in the "protected activity"; and

4. a causal connection can reasonably be inferred between the hostile action by the district and the person engaging in the "protected activity."

A good example of retaliation is the Office for Civil Rights decision in *Toledo Public Schools*, 42 IDELR 211 (OCR 2004). The mother of a student with a disability had been granted permission for an "out-of-district transfer." She needed the "out-of-district transfer" so that her son could remain in the school he was attending, even though the family had moved out of the school district.

The mother then tried to get special education services under the IDEA for her son. After she requested an evaluation to determine her son's eligibility for special education and looked into arranging district transportation for her son, the school district revoked her "out-of-district transfer." The letter revoking the "out-of-district transfer" stated that the school district was doing so because the mother had made numerous inquiries regarding transportation services for her son and had an outside agency investigate the school district (the mother had been helped by a caseworker who had contacted the school district on behalf of the mother).

> Section 504 and the ADA prohibit retaliation against a person with disabilities and persons acting on their behalf for trying to enforce their rights under these civil rights laws.

[272] 34 C.F.R. 104.61 and 28 C.F.R. 35.134(a) and (b)

After its investigation, OCR determined that the school district's revocation of the "out-of-district transfer" was retaliation and a violation of Section 504. The mother had (1) engaged in a "protected activity" - she had requested services under the IDEA; (2) the school district knew she had requested the services; (3) the district took an adverse action toward the mother by revoking the transfer; (4) there was a causal connection between the mother requesting IDEA services and the "out-of-district transfer" being revoked by the school district.

The anti-retaliation provisions of these disability civil rights laws also protect teachers and others who advocate on behalf of students with disabilities. In *Settlegood v. Portland Public Schools*, the Ninth Circuit Court of Appeals upheld a jury decision in favor of an adapted physical education teacher who filed a 504 claim after she was retaliated against because she criticized the school district's treatment of students with disabilities.[273]

The teacher had concerns about the way students with disabilities were treated by the school district. She was an itinerant teacher and had difficulty finding a place to teach her high school students. She also was concerned that material and equipment were often lacking, inadequate, or unsafe. After she expressed these concerns in a letter to her supervisors, her evaluations became much more negative and her probationary contract was not renewed. The teacher won monetary damages through a jury trial in federal district court and the decision was upheld by the Ninth Circuit Court of Appeals.

Note that in these two cases, the rights or "protected activities" being asserted were under the IDEA. The mother in the first case was trying to get her son determined eligible for IDEA services. The teacher in the second case was complaining about the inadequacy of IDEA services for her students. It is a violation of Section 504 and the ADA to retaliate against individuals for asserting rights under the IDEA as well as Section 504 and the ADA.

As with all cases, claims of retaliation do not always succeed. In *Walled Lake Public School District* 42 IDELR 144 (OCR 2004), the Office for Civil Rights concluded that a parent was not retaliated against when the school district prohibited her from being on school grounds after she had requested a due process hearing. After the parent requested the hearing, the school district's attorney sent her a letter telling her she should address all legal issues regarding the student to the attorney.

Later, the mother decided to withdraw her request for a hearing. She went to the school to deliver her letter to withdraw the hearing request. The mother asked the school receptionist to sign that the receptionist had received the letter. The receptionist, however, refused to accept the letter, telling the parent she should send it to the school district's attorney.

The parent told the Office for Civil Rights during its investigation that she became frustrated and angry, threw the letter on the receptionist's desk, and used an obscene word directed at two administrators who came to assist with the situation. Four days later the district's attorney sent the parent a letter telling her that because of this incident and some previous incidents of inappropriate behavior,

---

[273] *Settlegood v. Portland Public Schools*, 371 F.3d 503 (9th Cir. 2004), cert. denied, 125 S.Ct. 478 (U.S. 2004)

she was prohibited from being on any school district grounds without advance permission from the school district.

After its investigation, OCR determined that since the letter prohibiting the parent from district premises was sent nearly two months after the parent's hearing request, the prohibition was caused by her inappropriate behavior and not her request for a due process hearing. Thus, in this case, OCR determined that a key element in a complaint about retaliation was missing: a causal connection between the "protected activity" (requesting a due process hearing under the IDEA) and the "retaliation" (prohibiting the parent from being on district property without advance permission).

Community Access

Both Section 504 and the ADA require that school districts not discriminate against qualified persons with disabilities whether they are students, parents, or other community members. For example, both laws prohibit discrimination against persons with disabilities who are employees of the district or who are applying for employment with the district. Employers, including school districts, must provide reasonable accommodations to qualified persons with disabilities. If a person with a disability cannot perform an essential job function, then employers must consider accommodations that

would assist the person with a disability to perform the job function. Accommodations must be provided unless they create an undue hardship on the employer, in which case they are no longer reasonable.

Moreover, schools should be accessible, not just for students, but for employees and other members of the community with disabilities who work or attend functions in the schools. Parents, grandparents, and neighbors may have disabilities, but desire to attend activities at the school. Under both the ADA and Section 504, school **programs** must be accessible. To achieve accessibility, schools must identify architectural and communication barriers currently existing within their facilities. Those barriers must be removed, if their removal is readily achievable. The term "readily achievable" means that the barrier can be removed without much difficulty or expense.

Additionally, facilities that are going to be built must be constructed so that they are accessible and usable by persons with disabilities.[274] Also, if portions of existing buildings are altered, the alterations must be done so that the altered portion of the building is accessible.

> Remember that schools are not only for the students that attend them. Imagine a parent or grandparent who uses a wheelchair being unable to attend a school awards presentation where their child or grandchild is to receive an academic award because the school auditorium is inaccessible and the school administration did not relocate the ceremony.

---

[274] *North Bellmore Union Free School District* 35 IDELR 223 (OCR 2001) Student's need for air conditioned classroom was met by relocating entire class to air conditioned library during hot weather rather than air conditioning the classroom. *PEAKS Charter School* 35 IDELR 37 (OCR 2000) Charter school agreed to modify routes and entrances to buildings according to ADA guidelines as well as providing accessible parking.

Remember that schools are not only for the students that attend them. Imagine a parent or grandparent who uses a wheelchair being unable to attend a school awards presentation where their child or grandchild is to receive an academic award because the school auditorium is inaccessible and the school administration did not relocate the ceremony. Our schools are centers of community activities. Schools and school administrative buildings are often places where the community attends athletic contests, plays, school board meetings and other events. Finally, schools are also frequently where we vote. As community centers, schools should be accessible to all.

Notes:

Filing Complaints with the Office for Civil Rights

Individuals who believe they have been discriminated against by a school district in violation of Section 504 or the Americans with Disabilities Act may file complaints with the Office for Civil Rights within the United States Department of Education. Information regarding how to file a complaint and the complaint process can be obtained online at www.ed.gov/about/howto-index. This information is available on this website in English and Spanish as well as Arabic, Chinese, Farsi, Hindi, Hmong, Korean, Punjabi, Urdu, and Vietnamese. The OCR website, also a resource for more information on Section 504 and the ADA, is at www.ed.gov/policy/rights/guid/OCR/disabilityoverview.

Notes:

Back to the Beginning: Part C Early Intervention Services

Infants and Toddlers

Up to this point we have been discussing Part B of the IDEA that requires a free appropriate public education for students with disabilities from the ages of three to twenty-one (*school age children*). In this chapter we will discuss Part C of the IDEA--the requirements for states to provide early intervention services for children with disabilities from birth through age two. There are similarities to the requirements of Part B, serving school age students, and Part C, serving infants and toddlers. For example, both parts require child find, an individualized plan to direct services, and procedural safeguards. There are, however, important differences.

Part B services are primarily **student centered**. An Individualized Educational Program (IEP) is developed that focuses primarily on designing a program to meet the unique needs of the in-

dividual student with a disability. Under Part C Early Childhood Services an *Individualized Family Service Plan* (IFSP) is developed. The IFSP process emphasizes **services to meet the child's and family's needs and considers the resources, priorities and concerns of the family**.

Part B requires that students receive school services in the least restrictive environment. Part C requires that early intervention services be provided **in natural environments**.

Part B services are overseen by the State Education Agency and implemented by local education agencies, most often school districts. Under Part C, the governor of each state designates a **lead agency to implement early intervention services**. In some states that *lead agency* is the State Education Agency; in others it may be, for example, the Rehabilitation Agency, Health Department, Developmental

Disabilities Agency, or Social Services.[275] Part C services are delivered through a variety of agencies and local service providers in the community. Moreover, under Part C, the State must develop a statewide system to develop and deliver early intervention services to infants and toddlers.[276]

In reauthorizing Part C in the IDEA 2004, Congress found "that there is an urgent and substantial need

1. to enhance the development of infants and toddlers with disabilities, to minimize their potential for developmental delay, and to recognize the significant brain development that occurs during a child's first three years of life;

2. to reduce the educational costs to our society, including our Nations' schools, by minimizing the need for special education and related services after infants and toddlers reach school age;

3. to maximize the potential for individuals with disabilities to live independently in our society;

4. to enhance the capacity of families to meet the special needs of their infants and toddlers with disabilities; and

5. to enhance the capacity of State and local agencies and service providers to identify, evaluate, and meet the needs of all children, particularly minority, low-income,

inner city, and rural children, and infants and toddlers in foster care."[277]

Part C of the IDEA, therefore, provides early intervention services to infants and toddlers with disabilities. Those services are designed and delivered through an Individualized Family Service Plan (IFSP). The IFSP not only outlines services for the infant or toddler, but also services to assist the child's family.

Infant or Toddler with a Disability

Who are infants and toddlers with disabilities that are eligible for Part C early intervention services? An *infant or toddler with a disability* is a child under the age of three who needs early intervention services. The infant or toddler must need those services because the child (1) is experiencing developmental delays in one or more of the areas of cognitive development, physical development, communication development, social or emotional development, and adaptive development; or (2) has a diagnosed physical or mental condition that has a high probability of resulting in developmental delay.

Furthermore, the developmental delays the child is experiencing must be measured by appropriate diagnostic instruments and procedures. Finally, States may choose to serve at-risk infants and toddlers.[278] At-risk infants and toddlers are children under three years of age who would be at risk of experiencing a substantial developmental delay if early intervention services are not provided to the child.[279]

An infant or toddler with a disability is a child under the age of three who needs early intervention services.

[275] For more information on Part C and for a list of the Part C lead agencies see the National Early Intervention Technical Assistance Center website at www.nectac.org/partc.
[276] 20 U.S.C. 1431(b)
[277] 20 U.S.C. 1431(a)
[278] 20 U.S.C. 1432(5)(A)(B)
[279] 20 U.S.C. 1432(1)

Generally, like the IDEA's Part B, there are **two** elements to determine whether a child is an infant or toddler with a disability and eligible for Part C early intervention services. The child must (1) be experiencing developmental delays or have a condition that will probably result in a developmental delay, and (2) the child must need early intervention services.

Early Intervention Services

Part C provides early intervention services to children from birth through age two. Early intervention services are defined as developmental services that

1. are provided under public supervision;

2. are provided at no cost except where federal or state law provides for a system of payments by families, including a schedule of sliding fees;

3. are designed to meet the developmental needs of an infant or toddler with a disability, as identified by the individualized family service plan team, in any one or more of the following areas:

   a. physical development;

   b. cognitive development;

   c. communication development;

   d. social or emotional development; or

   e. adaptive development.[280]

Specific early intervention services can include

- family training, counseling, and home visits

- special instruction

- speech-language pathology and audiology services, and sign language and cued language services

- occupational therapy

- physical therapy

- psychological services

- service coordination services

- medical services for diagnostic and evaluation purposes

- early identification, screening, and assessment services

- health services necessary to enable the infant or toddler to benefit from other early intervention services

- social work services

- assistive technology devices and assistive technology services

- transportation and related costs that are necessary to enable an infant or toddler and the infant or toddler's family to receive any of these services.

These early intervention services are identified by the Individualized Family Service Plan (IFSP) team and included on the IFSP. The IFSP team is multidisciplinary, meaning the team includes individuals representing a range of disciplines or subjects. Parents are included as members of the IFSP team.[281]

---

[280] 20 U.S.C. 1432(4)(C)
[281] 20 U.S.C. 1436(a)(3)

Part C Service Providers

Early intervention services must be provided by people who are qualified in their area of expertise. Included as Part C service providers are

- special educators

- speech-language pathologists and audiologists

- occupational therapists

- physical therapists

- psychologists

- social workers

- nurses

- registered dieticians

- family therapists

- vision specialists, including ophthalmologists and optometrists

- orientation and mobility specialists and

- pediatricians and other physicians.[282]

Natural Environments

Part C services must be provided to the maximum extent appropriate in natural environments. Natural environments are settings like the child's home and community settings in which children without disabilities participate.[283] Serving infants and toddlers in their natural environment is similar to the requirement under the IDEA's Part B to serve school age students in the least restrictive environment.

[282] 20 U.S.C. 1432(4)(F)
[283] 20 U.S.C. 1432(4)(G)
[284] 20 U.S.C. 1435(16)(A)(B)
[285] 20 U.S.C. 1436(a)

Early intervention services must be provided in the appropriate natural environment, unless services cannot be achieved satisfactorily in a natural environment.[284] The idea in Part C is to try to provide services to infants and toddlers in their home and in other community settings that are routinely used by families rather than in clinics or doctor's and therapist's offices.

> Part C services must be provided to the maximum extent appropriate in natural environments. Natural environments are settings like the child's home and community settings in which children without disabilities participate.

Individualized Family Service Plan

The Individualized Family Service Plan (IFSP) is similar to the IEP developed under Part B for school age students. As noted above, the IFSP is written and developed by a multidisciplinary team that includes the child's parents. Before the IFSP is written the child will receive a multidisciplinary assessment. Multidisciplinary means that the assessment will include a range of subjects or disciplines. This evaluation will assess the child's strengths and needs and identify services to meet those needs.

In addition to an assessment of the child's strengths and needs, there will be a family-directed assessment of "the resources, priorities, and concerns of the family" as well as an "identification of the supports and services necessary to enhance the family's capacity to meet the development needs of the infant or toddler. . ."[285] Thus, Part C will look both at the child's needs and the resources, wishes, and concerns of the

> Thus, Part C will look both at the child's needs and the resources, wishes, and concerns of the family regarding services for their child. The IFSP can include services to support the family and the infant or toddler with a disability.

family regarding services for their child. The IFSP can include services to support the family and the infant or toddler with a disability.

Content of the Individualized Family Service Plan

The IFSP must be written and contain the following:

1. A statement of the infant's or toddler's present levels of physical development, cognitive development, communication development, social or emotional development, and adaptive development, based on objective criteria;

2. A statement of the family's resources, priorities, and concerns relating to enhancing the development of the family's infant or toddler with a disability;

3. A statement of the measurable results or outcomes expected to be achieved for the infant or toddler and the family, including preliteracy and language skills, as developmentally appropriate for the child, and the criteria, procedures, and timeline used to determine the degree to which progress toward achieving the results or outcomes is being made and whether modifications or revisions of the results or services are necessary;

4. A statement of specific early intervention services based on peer-reviewed research, to the extent practicable, necessary to meet the unique needs of the infant or toddler and the family, including frequency, intensity, and method of delivering services;

5. A statement of the natural environments in which early intervention services will appropriately be provided, including a justification of the extent, if any, to which the services will not be provided in a natural environment;

6. The projected dates for initiation of services and the anticipated length, duration, and frequency of the services;

7. The identification of the service coordinator from the profession most immediately relevant to the infant's or toddler's or family's needs (or which is otherwise qualified to carry out all applicable responsibilities under this part [Part C]) who will be responsible for the implementation of the plan and the coordination with other agencies and persons, including transition services; and

8. The steps to be taken to support the transition of the infant or toddler with a disability to preschool or other appropriate services.[286]

Parent Consent

After the IFSP is developed it must be fully explained to the child's parents. Before early intervention services are provided, the parents' written informed consent must be obtained. Part C specifically provides that if the parents do not

---

[286] 20 U.S.C. 1436(d)

consent to a particular intervention service, then it will not be provided.[287] Thus, parents have the right to consent to and accept only those early intervention services they wish their child and their family to receive, without jeopardizing receiving other early intervention services.[288]

> Thus, parents have the right to consent to and accept only those early intervention services they wish their child and their family to receive, without jeopardizing receiving other early intervention services.

Service Coordinator

The IFSP will identify a Service Coordinator to be responsible for implementing the plan. Early childhood services involve the efforts of a variety of local service providers and service agencies. It will be the Service Coordinator's job to coordinate those efforts to make sure the IFSP is implemented. The IFSP must be evaluated once a year and the family provided a review of the plan in six-month intervals. The plan can be reviewed more often based on the infant or toddler and family needs.[289]

The Service Coordinator will be responsible for ensuring the plan is re-evaluated and reviewed. The Service Coordinator is the family's primary link to their child's early intervention services. As the infant or toddler approaches the age of three (school age), planning must begin to transition the infant or toddler from Part C early intervention services. The infant

> The Service Coordinator is the family's primary link to their child's early intervention services.

or toddler may transition from Part C early intervention services to general education, or the infant or toddler may transition to Part B special education services. The Service Coordinator is responsible for coordinating the planning for that transition.

Transition from Part C Early Intervention Services

Transition from Part C early intervention services to school, preschool, other appropriate services, or leaving the Part C program is a major step for the infant, toddler and family. The transition should be smooth. There shouldn't be any gaps in services as the child reaches school age. Steps in transition include notifying the local education agency where the child resides that the infant or toddler will be reaching school age and may be eligible for Part B services.

If the child may be eligible for *preschool services* under Part B, a meeting should be held with the family, the lead agency for Part C, and the local

> Transition from Part C early intervention services to school, preschool, other appropriate services, or leaving the Part C program is a major step for the infant, toddler and family. The transition should be smooth. There shouldn't be any gaps in services as the child reaches school age.

---

[287] 20 U.S.C. 1436(e)
[288] 20 U.S.C. 1439(a)(3)
[289] 20 U.S.C. 1436(b)

education agency to discuss the Part B services the child may receive. Preschool services are school services provided to children with disabilities from the ages of three to five. The family must approve having this meeting, and it must be held no less than 90 days before the child is eligible for Part B services. Additionally, the family, Part C lead agency, and local education agency can choose to convene this meeting up to nine months before the infant or toddler becomes eligible for Part B school age services.[290]

Some children will not need special education services after leaving Part C early intervention services. For children who will not be eligible for Part B services, reasonable efforts need to be made to convene a similar meeting to discuss other appropriate services.[291]

As noted above, transition from early intervention services is a big step for infants, toddlers and families. During this transition, the responsibility for providing services to the child will transfer from the lead agency responsible for providing Part C services to the public schools. If the child, at the age of three, is a student with a disability and entitled to a free appropriate public education under the IDEA's Part B, the Individualized Educational Program process will be set in motion. To help smooth the transition, the parent can ask that the Part C Service Coordinator or other representative of the Part C system be invited to the initial IEP meeting.[292]

Procedural Safeguards

The Part C procedural safeguards outline minimum procedures that include the right to confidentiality; consent to or refusal of services; parent access to records or evaluations; procedures to protect the child's rights when the parents are not known or can't be found; prior notice

to parents of changes in services, assessment, or identification; and the timely resolution of parent complaints. The procedural safeguards under Part C regarding dispute resolution are not as prescriptive as the safeguards for school age students under Part B.

To be sure, the Part C procedures require the timely resolution of complaints by parents. The timely resolution of complaints regarding early intervention services is particularly important because the needs of infants and toddlers change rapidly. But the Part C procedures do not contain the lengthy prescriptive detail regarding the conduct of hearings that is contained in Part B. This is, no doubt, due to the statewide, multidisciplinary, and interagency nature of the system and the family-friendly focus of the early intervention process.

The Part B process for school age students focuses on school districts with parent input designing and delivering services. The Part C early intervention process focuses on coordinating the design and delivery of services to families through community agencies other than school districts. The Part C process involves special educators, but it involves providers from other disciplines as well. Other disciplines and agencies are often not as accustomed to formal dispute resolution procedures.

Moreover, Part C emphasizes working with and supporting **families to meet the needs of infants and toddlers**. Under Part C, the service plan includes statements of the family's resources, priorities, concerns and supports that meet the needs of the family as well as the in-

[290] 20 U.S.C. 1436(d)(8), 20 U.S.C. 1437(a)(9)(A)(i) (ii)(I)(II)
[291] 20 U.S.C. 1437(a)(9)(A)(ii)(III)
[292] 20 U.S.C. 1414(d)(1)(D)

fant or toddler. Part C acknowledges the right of parents to accept or decline services for their infant or toddler. While Part C anticipates that disagreements will occur in the early intervention process, Part C does not anticipate that the disagreements are as likely to be as adversarial as disputes under Part B for school age students have sometimes been.

Thus, the dispute resolution procedures under Part C, while requiring the timely administrative resolution of parent complaints, do not mandate a detailed due process hearing system. The lead agency in the state has some discretion or choice in how parent complaints are resolved. Families, advocates, and service providers should, therefore, contact the lead agency in their state for those procedures.[293]

Here is a more thorough list of the procedural safeguards required under Part C for Infants and Toddlers:

1. The timely administrative resolution of complaints by parents. Either side that disagrees with the resolution of the complaint may file a civil action (lawsuit) in state or federal district court.

2. The right to confidentiality of personally identifiable information including the right of parents to written notice and written consent to the exchange of personally identifiable information among agencies consistent with federal and state law.

3. The parents' right to determine if they will accept or decline any early inter-

vention services under Part C, in accordance with state law, without jeopardizing other early intervention services.

4. The opportunity for parents to examine records relating to assessment, screening, eligibility determinations, and the development of the IFSP.

5. Procedures to protect the rights of the infant or toddler whenever the parents of the infant or toddler are not known or cannot be found or the infant or toddler is a ward of the state. This includes assigning an individual to act as a surrogate for the child's parents.

6. Written prior notice to the parents of the infant or toddler whenever the state agency or service provider proposes to initiate or change the identification, evaluation, or placement of the infant or toddler. Written prior notice must also be provided if the state agency or service provider refuses to change the identification, evaluation or placement of the child.

7. Procedures designed to ensure that the notice in paragraph (6) fully informs the parents, in the parents' native language, of all the procedural safeguards, unless it is clearly not feasible to do so.

8. The parents' right to mediation according to the mediation procedures outlined in the procedural safeguards under Part B. (But where Part B refers to the State Education Agency and the local education agency, mediation under Part C should refer to the lead agency and the local service provider.)[294]

---

[293] Again, see the National Early Intervention Technical Assistance Center (NECTAC) website at www. nectac.org/partc. for more information on Part C and for a listing of the lead agencies in each state.

[294] 20 U.S.C. 1439(a)

Stay-put

Finally, while the Part C procedural safeguards are generally not as prescriptive as the safeguards under Part B, Part C does require that infants and toddlers continue to receive the appropriate early intervention services currently being provided during the complaint resolution process. If the infant or toddler is applying for initial services, then the services that are not being disputed will be provided. These provisions for stay-put will be true unless the parents and the state agency agree to another arrangement.[295]

Conclusion

Part C of the IDEA emphasizes involving the infant's or toddler's family in the design and delivery of services. Part C envisions a cooperative model of service delivery through a statewide system. The statewide system involves many community agencies and service providers in

> Part C of the IDEA emphasizes involving the infant's or toddler's family in the design and delivery of services. Part C envisions a cooperative model of service delivery through a statewide system.

delivering early intervention services. While Part C Early Intervention Services has some similarities to Part B, due to its family-friendly focus and involvement of local service providers and agencies that are not school districts, its complaint resolution procedures are less prescriptive. To be sure, the parents of infants and toddlers have significant procedural safeguards in the early intervention service delivery process, but Part C envisions a less adversarial process than the dispute resolution process provided under Part B for parents of school age students.

Notes:

---

[295] 20 U.S.C. 1439(b)

Notes:

X Facing Forward Looking Back

The history we've lived always seems so recent, but at the same time distant—so far away. So it is with the struggle for students with disabilities to go to school. The years have slipped by swiftly since Congress passed the Education for All Handicapped Children Act. That was a time when we held hope, promise, and opportunity precariously in our hands. While the Education for All Handicapped Children Act may not have fulfilled all our dreams, for most it ended the nightmare of days without school. While the IDEA may not have answered all our prayers, it delivered on many of its promises.

In the early days of the Education for All Handicapped Children Act, we argued over many questions that have since been settled in favor of students with disabilities receiving services and parents participating in the IEP process. Early questions were raised, like in the Ridge lawsuit, regarding whether children with

very severe disabilities were entitled to school services or could even attend public schools.

Other questions followed and, over time, were answered. Was providing physical, speech, and occupational therapy in institutions to children who could not walk or talk, education? Yes. Could children with disabilities be taught in temporary buildings, segregated from other students? No. Was catheterization or nursing

> While the Education for All Handicapped Children Act may not have fulfilled all our dreams, for most it ended the nightmare of days without school. While the IDEA may not have answered all our prayers, it delivered on many of its promises.

care a related service? Yes. Can schools place children based upon their "label," rather than their individual needs? No. Could students with disabilities be removed from regular classrooms for administrative convenience? No. As part of an appropriate education, are students entitled access to computers and augmentative communication devices needed educationally? Yes. Can children go to school in the summer if that's what's needed? Yes. Can parents be reimbursed for the tuition they've paid to private schools when the public schools have failed to serve their children? Yes. Are parents members of the IEP team? Yes. Can children with disabilities be expelled without school services for misbehavior? No. Now, all of those questions have been answered for students with disabilities, their parents, and their teachers.

So parents, students, teachers, legislators, and advocates should celebrate. Shout. High fives and take five. Smell the roses for a moment, but no laurel resting. Kids still need to be taught. Parents need to hear about the IDEA and stay current with its changes. Teachers need to teach and be taught. Individualized educational program teams must meet. Programs must be planned, put into practice, and reappraised. There will always be quarrels to be quelled and hearings to be held. Lessons to be learned. And every now and then there's talk about taking these rights away. There will always be work to be done—rights to be won.

Let's keep secure the gains we've made, while looking to new frontiers, always keeping our heads up while riding hard into that next horizon.

Notes:

Appendix A – **Sample Letter**

Request for Student Records

Your Name
Address
Date

Name of School Principal/Director of Special Education
School or District Name
Address (Street or P.O. Box Number)
City, State, Zip Code

RE: Student's Full Name
　　Birth date

Dear _____ :

　　Please consider this letter a written request to inspect (obtain copies of) the following items in my child's (student's name) educational records.

　　1.

　　2.

　　3.

　　I understand that I may be charged a reasonable fee to photocopy these records. Please notify me of the earliest date I may inspect these records. (Please send me copies of these records as soon as possible.) Thank you for your assistance.

Sincerely,

Your Name
Telephone Number

Appendix B – **Sample Letter**

Due Process Complaint Notice

Your Name
Address

Date

Superintendent
Name of School District/Local Education Agency
Address

Re: Due Process Complaint Notice for (Student's Name)

Dear Sir or Madam:

Please accept this letter as notice of a due process complaint.

    I. Complainant's Name:
        Your Name
        Student's Name
        Address and Telephone Number

   II. School the Child Attends:

 III. Name of Respondent:
        (Name of School Superintendent)
        Address and Telephone Number of the School District

        (Name of Director of Special Education)
        Address and Telephone Number

 IV. Date of Most Recent Violation:

        The most recent violation occurred on (date).

                Note: The IDEA 2004 requires that a due process hearing complaint must allege a violation that occurred not more than two years before the date the parent knew or should have known about the action that the parent is complaining about. This two-year timeline will apply unless the State has its own specific time limitation for filing due process complaint. [Sec. 615(b)(6)(B)]

V. Description of the Problem:

Describe the problem regarding the proposed initiation or change that you are complaining about. Be sure to include specific facts that describe and relate to the problem. A complaint can be made regarding "any matter relating to the identification, evaluation, or educational placement of the child, or the provision of a free appropriate public education to such child." [Sec. 615(b)(6)(A)]

VI. Proposed Resolution:

Describe what you want to resolve the problem. For example: If the problem regards the IEP not requiring a related service such as speech therapy or physical therapy, a proposed resolution might be that the school district provide the speech therapy or physical therapy.

Respectfully submitted:

Your name and telephone number

cc   Name of the Director of Special Education
     State Education Agency (**Note that a copy of the Due Process Complaint Notice must be forwarded to the State Education Agency.**)

Note: The IDEA 2004 requires that the each State Education Agency develop a model form to assist parents in filing a complaint and due process complaint notice. While this form includes the IDEA 2004 requirements for the basic contents of a due process complaint notice, you should check with your State Education Agency for your state's model form. You may also want to consult with an attorney regarding drafting a notice that describes your specific complaint.

Appendix C

UNITED STATES DEPARTMENT OF EDUCATION
WASHINGTON, D.C. 20202

July 25, 2000

Dear Colleague:

On behalf of the Office for Civil Rights (OCR) and the Office of Special Education and Rehabilitative Services (OSERS) in the U.S. Department of Education, we are writing to you about a vital issue that affects students in school – harassment based on disability. Our purpose in writing is to develop greater awareness of this issue, to remind interested persons of the legal and educational responsibilities that institutions have to prevent and appropriately respond to disability harassment, and to suggest measures that school officials should take to address this very serious problem. This letter is not an exhaustive legal analysis. Rather, it is intended to provide a useful overview of the existing legal and educational principles related to this important issue.

Why Disability Harassment Is Such an Important Issue

Through a variety of sources, both OCR and OSERS have become aware of concerns about disability harassment in elementary and secondary schools and colleges and universities. In a series of conference calls with OSERS staff, for example, parents, disabled persons, and advocates for students with disabilities raised disability harassment as an issue that was very important to them. OCR's complaint workload has reflected a steady pace of allegations regarding this issue, while the number of court cases involving allegations of disability harassment has risen. OCR and OSERS recently conducted a joint focus group where we heard about the often devastating effects on students of disability harassment that ranged from abusive jokes, crude name-calling, threats, and bullying, to sexual and physical assault by teachers and other students.

We take these concerns very seriously. Disability harassment can have a profound impact on students, raise safety concerns, and erode efforts to ensure that students with disabilities have equal access to the myriad benefits that an education offers. Indeed, harassment can seriously interfere with the ability of students with disabilities to receive the education critical to their advancement. We are committed to doing all that we can to help prevent and respond to disability harassment and lessen the harm of any harassing conduct that has occurred. We seek your support in a joint effort to address this critical issue and to promote such efforts among educators who deal with students daily.

What Laws Apply to Disability Harassment

Schools, colleges, universities, and other educational institutions have a responsibility to ensure equal educational opportunities for all students, including students with disabilities. This responsibility is based on Section 504 of the Rehabilitation Act of 1973 (Section 504) and Title II of the Americans with Disabilities Act of 1990 (Title II), which are enforced by OCR. Section 504 covers all schools, school districts, and colleges and universities receiving federal funds.[1] Title II covers all state and local entities, including school districts and public institutions of higher education, whether or not they receive federal funds.[2] Disability harassment is a form of discrimination prohibited by Section 504 and Title II.[3] Both Section 504 and Title II provide parents and students with grievance procedures and due process remedies at the local level. Individuals and organizations also may file complaints with OCR.

States and school districts also have a responsibility under Section 504, Title II, and the Individuals with Disabilities Education Act (IDEA),[4] which is enforced by OSERS, to ensure that a free appropriate public education (FAPE) is made available to eligible students with disabilities. Disability harassment may result in a denial of FAPE under these statutes. Parents may initiate administrative due process procedures under IDEA, Section 504, or Title II to address a denial of FAPE, including a denial that results from disability harassment. Individuals and organizations also may file complaints with OCR, alleging a denial of FAPE that results from disability harassment. In addition, an individual or organization may file a complaint alleging a violation of IDEA under separate procedures with the state educational agency.[5] State compliance with IDEA, including compliance with FAPE requirements, is monitored by OSERS' Office of Special Education Programs (OSEP).

Harassing conduct also may violate state and local civil rights, child abuse, and criminal laws. Some of these laws may impose obligations on educational institutions to contact or coordinate with state or local agencies or police with respect to disability harassment in some cases; failure to follow appropriate

---

[1] Section 504 provides: "No otherwise qualified individual with a disability . . . shall, solely by reason of her or his disability, be excluded from the participation in, be denied the benefits of, or be subjected to discrimination under any program or activity receiving federal financial assistance." 29 U.S.C. § 794(a). See 34 CFR Part 104 (Section 504 implementing regulations).

[2] Title II provides that "no qualified individual with a disability shall, by reason of such disability, be excluded from participation in or be denied the benefits of the services, programs, or activities of a public entity, or be subjected to discrimination by any such entity." 42 U.S.C. § 12132. See 28 CFR Part 35 (Title II implementing regulations).

[3] The Department of Education's Office for Civil Rights (OCR) has issued policy guidance on discriminatory harassment based on race (see 59 Fed. Reg. 11448 (Mar. 10, 1994), http://www.ed.gov/offices/OCR/race394.html) and sex (see 62 Fed Reg. 12034 (Mar. 13, 1997), http://www.ed.gov/offices/OCR/sexhar00.html. These policies make clear that school personnel who understand their legal obligations to address harassment are in the best position to recognize and prevent harassment, and to lessen the harm to students if, despite their best efforts, harassment occurs. In addition, OCR recently collaborated with the National Association of Attorneys General (NAAG) to produce a guide to raise awareness of, and provide examples of effective practices for dealing with, hate crimes and harassment in schools, including harassment based on disability. See "Protecting Students from Harassment and Hate Crime, A Guide for Schools," U.S. Department of Education, Office for Civil Rights, and the National Association of Attorneys General (Jan. 1999) (OCR/NAAG Harassment Guide), Appendix A: Sample School Policies. The OCR/NAAG Harassment Guide may be accessed on the internet at http://www.ed.gov/pubs/Harassment. These documents are a good resource for understanding the general principle of discriminatory harassment. The policy guidance on sexual harassment will be clarified to explain how OCR's longstanding regulatory requirements continue to apply in this area in light of recent Supreme Court decisions addressing the sexual harassment of students.

[4] 20 U.S.C. §1400 et seq.

[5] 34 C.F.R. § 300.660 et seq.

procedures under these laws could result in action against an educational institution. Many states and educational institutions also have addressed disability harassment in their general anti-harassment policies.[6]

Disability Harassment May Deny a Student an Equal Opportunity to Education under Section 504 or Title II

Disability harassment under Section 504 and Title II is intimidation or abusive behavior toward a student based on disability that creates a hostile environment by interfering with or denying a student's participation in or receipt of benefits, services, or opportunities in the institution's program. Harassing conduct may take many forms, including verbal acts and name-calling, as well as nonverbal behavior, such as graphic and written statements, or conduct that is physically threatening, harmful, or humiliating.

When harassing conduct is sufficiently severe, persistent, or pervasive that it creates a hostile environment, it can violate a student's rights under the Section 504 and Title II regulations. A hostile environment may exist even if there are no tangible effects on the student where the harassment is serious enough to adversely affect the student's ability to participate in or benefit from the educational program. Examples of harassment that could create a hostile environment follow.

- Several students continually remark out loud to other students during class that a student with dyslexia is "retarded" or "deaf and dumb" and does not belong in the class; as a result, the harassed student has difficulty doing work in class and her grades decline.

- A student repeatedly places classroom furniture or other objects in the path of classmates who use wheelchairs, impeding the classmates' ability to enter the classroom.

- A teacher subjects a student to inappropriate physical restraint because of conduct related to his disability, with the result that the student tries to avoid school through increased absences.[7]

- A school administrator repeatedly denies a student with a disability access to lunch, field trips, assemblies, and extracurricular activities as punishment for taking time off from school for required services related to the student's disability.

- A professor repeatedly belittles and criticizes a student with a disability for using accommodations in class, with the result that the student is so discouraged that she has great difficulty performing in class and learning.

- Students continually taunt or belittle a student with mental retardation by mocking and intimidating him so he does not participate in class.

---

[6] For more information regarding the requirements of state and local laws, consult the OCR/NAAG Harassment Guide, cited in footnote 3 above.

[7] Appropriate classroom discipline is permissible, generally, if it is of a type that is applied to all students or is consistent with the Individuals with Disabilities Education Act (IDEA) and Section 504, including the student's Individualized Education Program or Section 504 plan.

When disability harassment limits or denies a student's ability to participate in or benefit from an educational institution's programs or activities, the institution must respond effectively. Where the institution learns that disability harassment may have occurred, the institution must investigate the incident(s) promptly and respond appropriately.

Disability Harassment Also May Deny a Free Appropriate Public Education

Disability harassment that adversely affects an elementary or secondary student's education may also be a denial of FAPE under the IDEA, as well as Section 504 and Title II. The IDEA was enacted to ensure that recipients of IDEA funds make available to students with disabilities the appropriate special education and related services that enable them to access and benefit from public education. The specific services to be provided a student with a disability are set forth in the student's individualized education program (IEP), which is developed by a team that includes the student's parents, teachers and, where appropriate, the student. Harassment of a student based on disability may decrease the student's ability to benefit from his or her education and amount to a denial of FAPE.

How to Prevent and Respond to Disability Harassment

Schools, school districts, colleges, and universities have a legal responsibility to prevent and respond to disability harassment. As a fundamental step, educational institutions must develop and disseminate an official policy statement prohibiting discrimination based on disability and must establish grievance procedures that can be used to address disability harassment.[8] A clear policy serves a preventive purpose by notifying students and staff that disability harassment is unacceptable, violates federal law, and will result in disciplinary action. The responsibility to respond to disability harassment, when it does occur, includes taking prompt and effective action to end the harassment and prevent it from recurring and, where appropriate, remedying the effects on the student who was harassed.

The following measures are ways to both prevent and eliminate harassment:

- Creating a campus environment that is aware of disability concerns and sensitive to disability harassment; weaving these issues into the curriculum or programs outside the classroom.

- Encouraging parents, students, employees, and community members to discuss disability harassment and to report it when they become aware of it.

- Widely publicizing anti-harassment statements and procedures for handling discrimination complaints, because this information makes students and employees aware of what constitutes harassment, that such conduct is prohibited, that the institution will not tolerate such behavior, and that effective action, including disciplinary action, where appropriate, will be taken.

---

[8] Section 504 (at 34 CFR § 104.7) and Title II (at 28 CFR § 35.107(a)) require that institutions have published internal policies and grievance procedures to address issues of discrimination on the basis of disability, which includes disability harassment. While there need not be separate grievance procedures designed specifically for disability harassment, the grievance procedures that are available must be effective in resolving problems of this nature.

- Providing appropriate, up-to-date, and timely training for staff and students to recognize and handle potential harassment.

- Counseling both person(s) who have been harmed by harassment and person(s) who have been responsible for the harassment of others.

- Implementing monitoring programs to follow up on resolved issues of disability harassment.

- Regularly assessing and, as appropriate, modifying existing disability harassment policies and procedures for addressing the issue, to ensure effectiveness.

Technical Assistance Is Available

U.S. Secretary of Education Richard Riley has emphasized the importance of ensuring that schools are safe and free of harassment. Students can not learn in an atmosphere of fear, intimidation, or ridicule. For students with disabilities, harassment can inflict severe harm. Teachers and administrators must take emphatic action to ensure that these students are able to learn in an atmosphere free from harassment.

Disability harassment is preventable and can not be tolerated. Schools, colleges, and universities should address the issue of disability harassment not just when but **before** incidents occur. As noted above, awareness can be an important element in preventing harassment in the first place.

The Department of Education is committed to working with schools, parents, disability advocacy organizations, and other interested parties to ensure that no student is ever subjected to such conduct, and that where such conduct occurs, prompt and effective action is taken. For more information, you may contact OCR or OSEP through 1-800-USA-LEARN or 1-800-437-0833 for TTY services. You also may directly contact one of the OCR enforcement offices listed on the enclosure or OSEP, by calling (202) 205-5507 or (202) 205-5465 for TTY services.

Thank you for your attention to this serious matter.

Norma V. Cantu,
Assistant Secretary for
Civil Rights

Judith E. Heumann,
Assistant Secretary
Office of Special Education
and Rehabilitative Services

Appendix D – **Glossary and Acronyms**

Assistive Technology (AT): An AT device is any item, piece of equipment, or product or system, whether acquired commercially or off the shelf, modified, or customized, that is used to increase, maintain, or improve functional capabilities of a child with a disability. It does not include medical devices that are surgically implanted. An AT service is any service that directly assists a child with a disability in the selection, acquisition, or use of an AT device.

Behavior Intervention Plan (BIP): The behavioral intervention plan describes interventions and modifications designed to change a student's behavior that is causing concern and teach new more appropriate behaviors. A behavioral intervention plan is based on information gathered through a **functional behavioral assessment (FBA)**.

Child Find: Child find is the requirement that State Education Agencies (for children in the state) and local education agencies (for children living in the jurisdiction) locate and refer for evaluation children from birth to age 21 who may need special education services under the IDEA.

Child with a Disability: Under the IDEA a child with a disability is a child (A) with mental retardation, hearing impairments (including deafness), speech or language impairments, visual impairments (including blindness), serious emotional disturbance, orthopedic impairments, autism, traumatic brain injury, other health impairments, or specific learning disabilities; and (B) who, because the child has an impairment, needs special education and related services. Under Section 504 a child has a disability if the child has a mental or physical disability that substantially limits one or more major life activities.

Early Intervention Services: Early intervention services are services provided to infants and toddlers (children aged birth through two) under Part C of the IDEA. Early intervention services are delivered according to an Individualized Family Service Plan (IFSP).

Free Appropriate Public Education (FAPE): (1) Under the IDEA, Free Appropriate Public Education means special education and related services provided at public expense according to an Individualized Educational Program (IEP).

(2) **Under Section 504 of the Rehabilitation Act** a free appropriate public education means providing regular or special education services to meet the individual education needs of children with disabilities as adequately as the needs of children without disabilities are met.

Functional Behavioral Assessment (FBA): A functional behavioral assessment gathers information about a student's behavior to try to determine what function, or purpose, the behavior serves for the student. The functional behavioral assessment is then used to develop a **behavioral intervention plan** sometimes referred to as a **BIP**.

Individualized Educational Program (IEP): An IEP is a written educational plan developed by a team that lists the specific services a student with a disability will be provided in order to receive a free appropriate public education. The IEP team includes the parent, appropriate school personnel (including a regular education teacher if the student is receiving services in regular education or it is anticipated the student may be receiving services in regular education), and other individuals who know about the student and the student's educational needs.

Individualized Family Service Plan (IFSP): An IFSP is a written plan to deliver early childhood services to an infant or toddler with a disability. The IFSP is developed by a multidisciplinary team that includes the child's parents.

Infant and Toddler with a Disability: An infant or toddler with a disability is a child under 3 years of age who is eligible for early intervention services.

Interim Alternative Educational Setting (IAES): The interim alternative educational setting is a setting in which a student with a disability may be placed under certain circumstances during the disciplinary process. The IAES is determined by the IEP team and must provide educational services to enable the student to continue to participate in the general education curriculum and progress toward meeting goals in the student's IEP.

Lead Agency: Under the IDEA, the lead agency in a state is the agency responsible for overseeing and supervising the implementation of Part C early childhood services for infants and toddlers.

Least Restrictive Environment (LRE): The least restrictive environment is the requirement that students with disabilities be educated in regular classrooms with students without disabilities to the maximum extent appropriate. Students with disabilities should only be placed in special classes or separate schools if it is determined that, even with the provision of supplementary aids and services, the regular classroom placement will not be successful. Part C of the IDEA, providing early intervention services to infants and toddlers with disabilities, has a similar requirement but uses the term **natural environments** rather than least restrictive environment. Natural environments, under Part C, means providing early intervention services to the infant or toddler in the home and other community settings in which children without disabilities participate to the maximum extent appropriate.

Local Education Agency (LEA): A local education agency is a public board of education or other authority in a state that controls or directs public elementary and secondary schools in a city, county, township, school district or other political subdivision of a state. It can also be a combination of school districts or counties that the state recognizes as the administrative agency for local public schools. The local education agency is responsible for implementing the IDEA on the local level. In this book the term "school district" is generally used for the term "local education agency."

Manifestation Determination: The manifestation determination is a decision made by a student's parents, local education agency, and relevant members of the IEP team regarding whether a student's misbehavior that violates a code of student conduct is related to the student's disability. Which members of the IEP team are "relevant" is determined by the student's parents and the local education agency.

Parent: Under the IDEA the term parent means—(A) a natural, adoptive, or foster parent of a child (unless the foster parent is prohibited under state law from serving as a parent); (B) a guardian (but not the state if the child is a ward of the state); (C) an individual acting in the place of a natural or adoptive parent (including a grandparent, stepparent, or other relative) with whom the child lives, or an individual who is legally responsible for the child's welfare; or (D) a surrogate parent.

Parentally-placed Private School Children with Disabilities: Children with disabilities who are enrolled by their parents in private schools, including religious schools.

Preschool Services: Preschool services are special education and related services provided to children with disabilities from the ages of 3 to 5. Preschool children with disabilities are entitled to services under Part B of the IDEA and are considered school age.

School Age Children: Children between the ages of 3 and 21. School age children with disabilities are entitled to a free appropriate public education under Part B of the IDEA.

Services Plan: A plan that describes the special education and related services the school district will provide to a parentally-placed child with a disability who is enrolled in a private school and has been designated to receive services.

State Education Agency (SEA): State Education Agency means the state board of education or other agency in the state that is primarily responsible for the state supervision of public elementary and secondary schools. The State Education Agency is responsible for ensuring that children with disabilities receive a free appropriate public education throughout the State.

Supplementary Aids and Services: Supplementary aids and services means aids, services and other supports that are provided in regular education classes or other education-related settings to enable children with disabilities to be educated with children without disabilities to the maximum extent appropriate.

Surrogate Parent: A surrogate parent is an individual who is appointed to protect the educational rights of a child with a disability when the child's parents are not known or cannot be located.

Appendix E – **Circuit Courts**

1st Circuit
- Maine
- Massachusetts
- New Hampshire
- Puerto Rico
- Rhode Island

2nd Circuit
- Connecticut
- New York
- Vermont

3rd Circuit
- Delaware
- New Jersey
- Pennsylvania
- Virgin Islands

4th Circuit
- Maryland
- North Carolina
- South Carolina
- Virginia
- West Virginia

5th Circuit
- Louisiana
- Mississippi
- Texas

6th Circuit
- Kentucky
- Michigan
- Ohio
- Tennessee

7th Circuit
- Illinois
- Indiana
- Wisconsin

8th Circuit
- Arkansas
- Iowa
- Minnesota
- Missouri
- Nebraska
- North Dakota
- South Dakota

9th Circuit
- Alaska
- Arizona
- California
- Guam
- Hawaii
- Idaho
- Montana
- Nevada
- Northern Mariana Islands
- Oregon
- Washington

10th Circuit
- Colorado
- Kansas
- New Mexico
- Oklahoma
- Utah
- Wyoming

11th Circuit
- Alabama
- Florida
- Georgia

DC Circuit
- Washington, DC

Index

The Legal Center for People
with Disabilities [C] and Older People

Colorado's Protection & Advocacy System

About our organization . . .

The Legal Center is a nonprofit organization protecting the human, civil and legal rights of people with disabilities and older people established in 1976. As Colorado's Protection and Advocacy System, The Legal Center has authority under federal law to gain access to facilities and records in order to investigate allegations of abuse and neglect. The organization also helps people obtain state and federally funded services, such as special education, mental health services, developmental disabilities services, and vocational rehabilitation. The Legal Center specializes in civil rights and discrimination issues.

The Legal Center promotes systemic change to sustain or improve the quality of life for children and adults with disabilities and senior citizens. The Legal Center provides direct legal representation, education, advocacy and legislative analysis to promote the independence, self-determination, empowerment and community participation of its clients.

Similar organizations exist in every state and territory as part of a national protection and advocacy network.

About the author . . .

Randy Chapman came to The Legal Center in 1977 as a Volunteer in Service to America (VISTA). He was newly graduated from law school at the University of Texas at Austin. A year later he was hired as a staff attorney. He has been the Director of Legal Services since 1980.

He played a pivotal role in the development of disability law and he helped break ground in implementing special education law.

His influence is reflected in Colorado statute and policy. In the developmental disabilities area, he established Human Rights Committees in legislation to review medications, behavioral programs, and ensure investigation of abuse and neglect. He added the requirement that people with developmental disabilities be represented on the boards of directors of community service organizations. He also drafted the due process language in the state statute and had significant input in the development of the Colorado Department of Education's complaint process for children in special education.

He has overseen legal representation to more than 10,000 people with disabilities in Colorado and made more than 500 presentations on disability law. In 1998 he was awarded the Martin Luther King Jr. Humanitarian Award by the Martin Luther King Jr. Colorado Holiday Commission. He is also the author of numerous articles, two video scripts, *Assistive Technology: Universe of Opportunities*, and *The New Handbook for Special Education Rights*.

He lives in Golden, Colorado, with his wife and two sons.